The Breval
Cello Sonata in C Major

Practice Edition

A Learn Cello Practically Book

Written and Compiled by Cassia Harvey
based on the Sonata by Jean-Baptiste Bréval

Grateful thanks to Clara Lee for her help in preparing this manuscript!

CHP371

©2021 by C. Harvey Publications All Rights Reserved.

www.charveypublications.com - print books
www.learnstrings.com - PDF downloadable books
www.harveystringarrangements.com - chamber music

Table of Contents

Section	Page
What's In the Book	3
How to Practice Using This Edition	4
Understanding Symbols and Terms	5
Reading and Playing Half and Whole Steps	6
Extending Past First Position to Reach More Notes	7
How the Positions Intersect on the A and D Strings	8
How the Positions Intersect on the G and C Strings	9
Preparing to Play Breval	10
Movement One - Preparatory Exercises, Right Hand	11
Positions Used in the Breval Sonata (with pictures)	33
About Trills	36
Movement One - Preparatory Exercises, Left Hand	37
What to Focus on in Movement One/Tempos	55
Movement One - With Study Notes	56
Movement Two - Preparatory Exercises, Right Hand	60
Movement Two - Preparatory Exercises, Left Hand	71
What to Focus on in Movement Two/Tempos	79
Movement Two - With Study Notes	80

Sonata in C Major - Complete Piece
- Movement One … 84
- Movement Two … 86

Sonata in C Major - Cello Duet (from Schroeder version)
- Movement One … 88
- Movement Two … 92

Sonata in C Major - Piano Accompaniment
- Movement One … 96
- Movement Two … 100

Sonata in C Major - Cello Duet (from Manuscript)
- Movement One … 104
- Movement Two … 108

Cello Curriculum Segments - Where to Place Breval … 112

What's In the Book

How to Practice Using This Edition
These pages have ideas for developing a practice strategy to learn the Sonata. From explanations of symbols and terms to a description of half and whole steps, these pages tell you how the book can be most helpful to you.

Preparatory Exercises
The most difficult parts in the Sonata were identified and then broken down and taught in these pages. The Preparatory Exercises for each movement are followed by the "Movement with Study Notes."

Movements With Study Notes
Each movement of the Sonata is written with notes for study, including marked positions, some beat marks, and extension reminders.

Complete Sonata
The entire cello part to the Sonata is here, for practice or performance.

Sonata with Cello Duet Part
Carl Schroeder made some changes to the Breval Sonata that are commonly played today. This book includes two duet version: a Schroeder-compatible version and the cello duet part that Breval originally wrote (included without edits.)

Piano Accompaniment
The piano accompaniment, composed by C. Schroeder, is included for study, practice, or performance.

Cello Curriculum Segment - Where to Place Romberg
These pages show how the Breval Cello Sonata in C Major can fit in a cello curriculum, along with recommended methods, etudes, and supplemental study books.

©2021 C. Harvey Publications All Rights Reserved.

How to Practice Using This Edition

1. Play and master the **Preparatory Exercises** for each movement. A preparatory exercise may be followed by the excerpt it is teaching, labeled "**Excerpt**". Repeat the excerpt until it feels comfortable.

2. You may also, at the same time, practice the piece using the **Movement with Study Notes** that follows each set of Preparatory Exercises.

3. Once you have learned the movement fairly well, transition to the same movement in the **Complete Piece** section (pages 84-87) or the **Duet** section (pages 88-93.)

4. The entire book can be played with free **Play-Along** files. See below for more information.

5. Play the **Sonata with Cello Duet** part with your teacher or with another cellist. The duet is also included in original form, copied directly from the manuscript, at the end of the book, on page 104.

6. If desired, you may play the Sonata with the included **Piano Accompaniment**.

7. See what to play next in a typical cello curriculum, using the lists at the end of the book.

Play-Along Sound Files

Play-Along Sound Files for this book can be found at https://soundcloud.com/charveypublications/sets/the-breval-cello-sonata-in-c.

The files are listed according to their page in the book.

Soundcloud can be accessed on your computer or on your mobile device, via their free app. The files may be streamed or downloaded to your device.

©2021 C. Harvey Publications All Rights Reserved.

Understanding Symbols and Terms

In this book, **Roman Numerals** indicate strings — never positions.
I = A string, II = D string, III = G string, IV = C string

> **Small counting notes** are sometimes included over the written notes to help you learn how to play the rhythms correctly.
>
>
>
> Sometimes the counting notes help you subdivide, or break the beats down into smaller counts:

Positions are indicated by numbers and words: 4th position, 3rd position, etc. Pages 8 and 9 show you how the positions intersect. Pages 33-35 have picures of the left hand in the different positions used in the Breval Sonata.

> *Extend* refers to reaching two whole steps with the fingers of the left hand. If you have not learned extensions yet, see a method such as Cello Stretching: Extended First Position (CHP243.) *Occasionally, an arrow will be used to remind you to extend forward or backward.*
> *Closed* refers to a regular position, where the hand is not extending. See page 7 for more information on extending.

Metronome markings are included before the *Movements with Study Notes* for both study and performance tempos. They are listed as a range (i.e. from 72-88.) After initially learning the notes in the Sonata, you might want to continue your practice with the metronome, starting at the slowest listed tempo (or even slower.) As you progress, move the metronome up one or two notches and keep practicing. Continue getting faster until you reach the performance tempo where you feel most comfortable. Metronome markings are only approximate; feel free to play the piece at a slower or faster tempo!

Reading and Playing Half and Whole Steps

Here are some practical ways to think of steps on the cello:
- The space between each finger in the regular (closed) lower positions is a half step.
- The space between three fingers (for instance, 1st finger and 3rd finger) in regular (closed) lower positions is a whole step.
- To reach a whole step with 1st and 2nd fingers, you must extend or stretch. *In this case, the thumb should move up under 2nd finger to allow you to reach easily.*
- As you move up through the positions, the spaces between the notes get smaller. A half step in first position will be a little bit bigger than a half step in fourth position.

Half steps are marked this way:

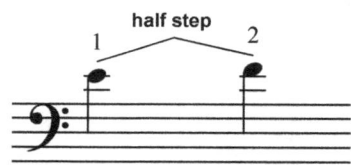

Half step space

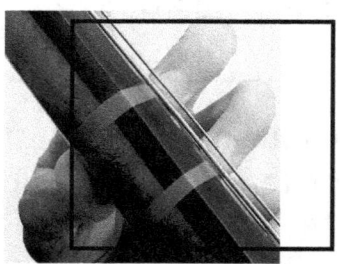

Whole steps are marked this way:

Whole step space with 1st and 3rd finger (closed postion.)

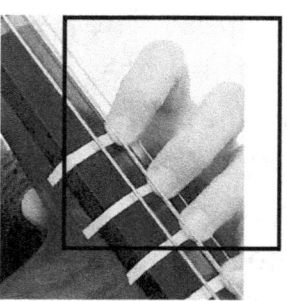

Whole step space with 1st and 2nd finger (extended position.)

Extending Past First Position to Reach More Notes

In order to reach two whole steps with the fingers of the left hand, you need to extend, or stretch, your 1st finger so that it is a whole step away from the 2nd finger.

In extensions, the thumb must be under the second finger to allow the hand to open up fully!

If the thumb is behind the first finger, the hand will usually not be able to reach the full stretch and play the notes in tune.

©2021 C. Harvey Publications All Rights Reserved.

How the Positions Intersect on the A and D Strings

A string

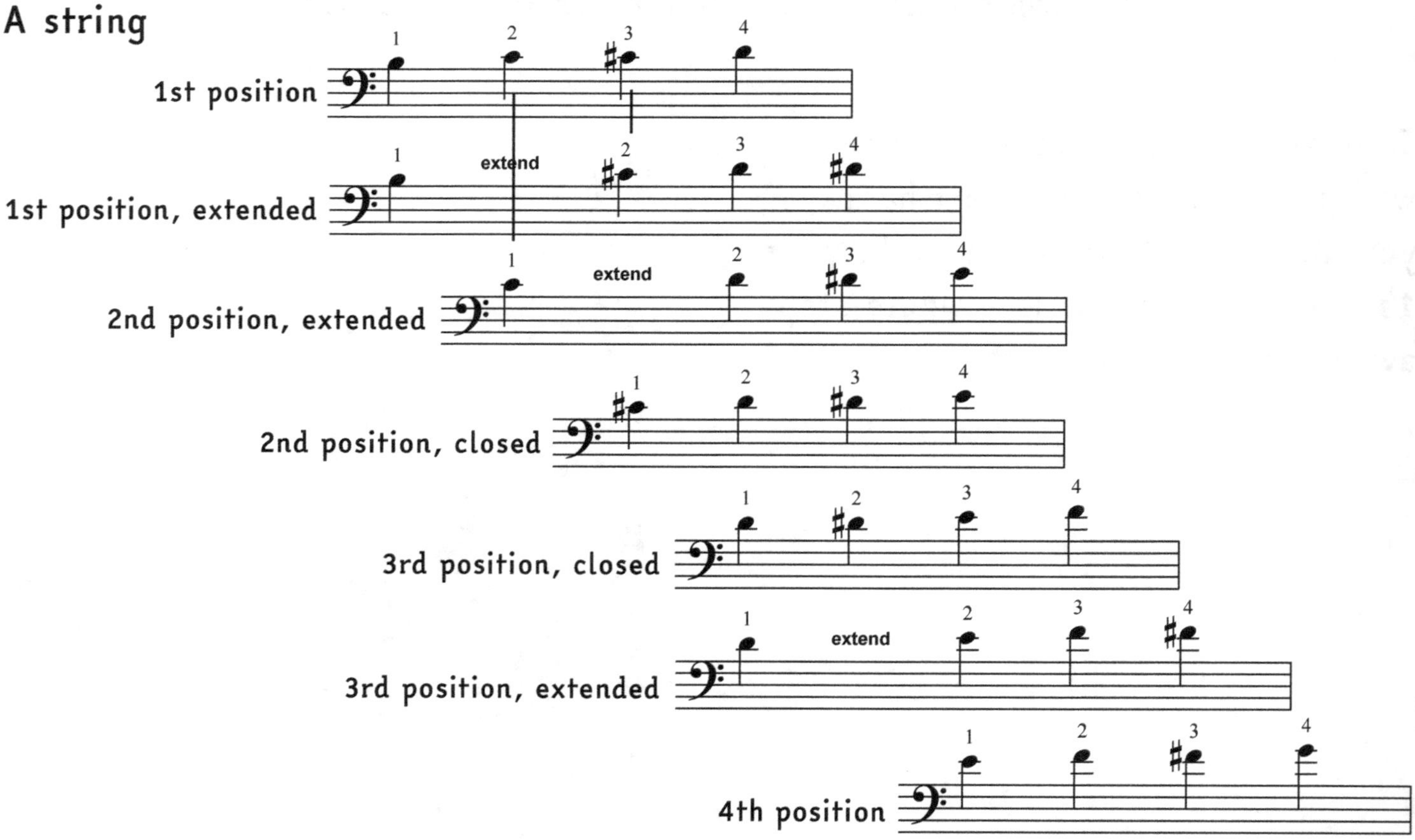

D string

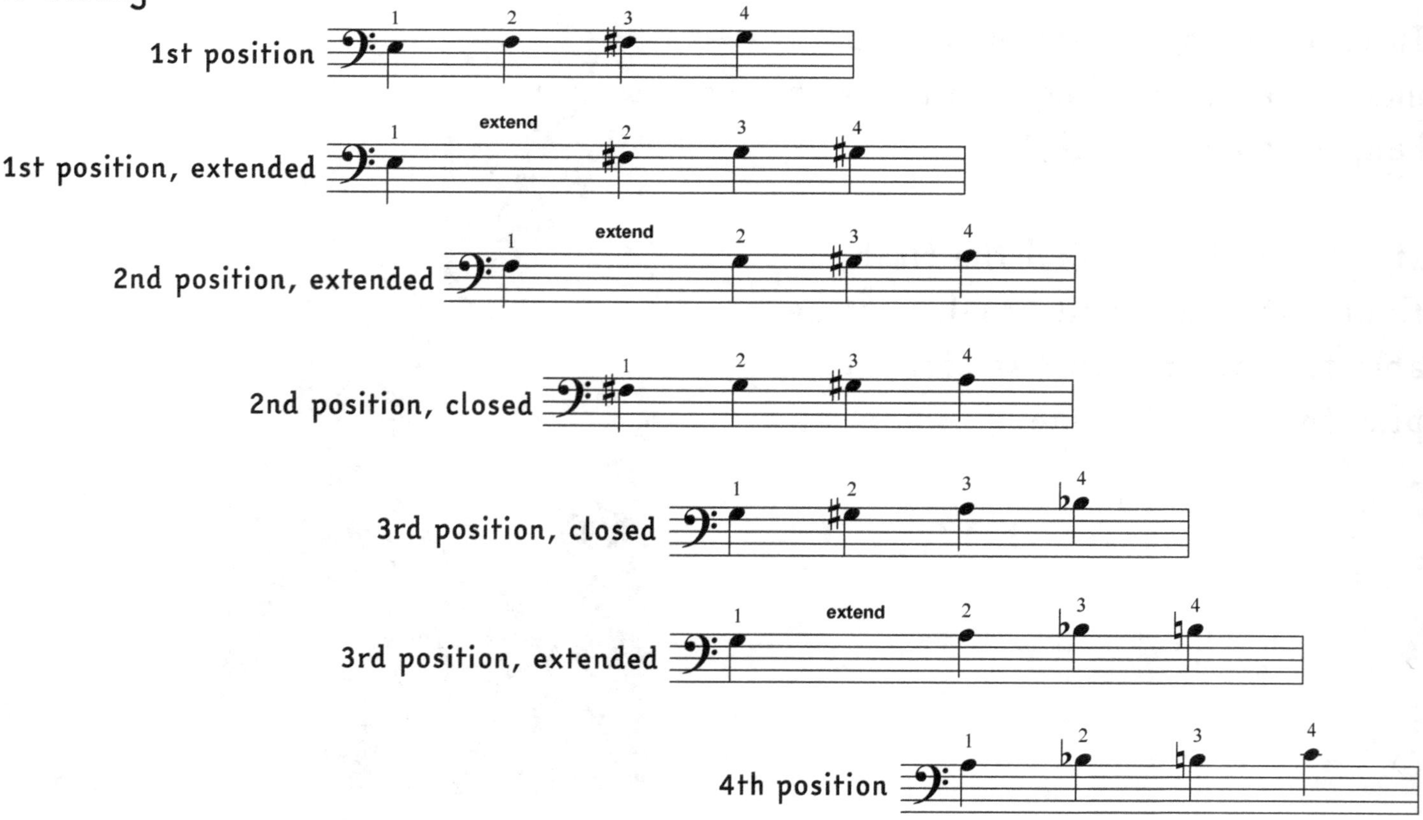

How the Positions Intersect on the G and C Strings

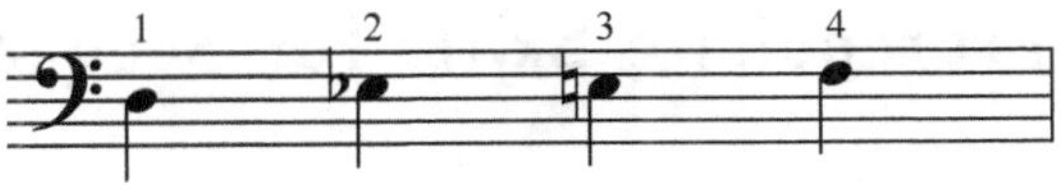

©2021 C. Harvey Publications   All Rights Reserved.

Preparing for Breval

Prerequisite Skills for First Movement

- Ability to read and play both closed and extended first position.
- Ability to read, shift to, and play in fourth position (including mid-string harmonic.)
- Ability to read, shift to, and play in basic second and third position.
- Some familiarity with half position.
- Ability to play triplets, dotted quarter and eighth notes.
- Ability to play a 2-Octave C major scale, a 2-Octave D major scale, and a 2-Octave G major scale.

Prerequisite Skills for Second Movement

- See skills above.
- Ability to play in a 6/8 time signature, including knowing how to count sixteenth, eighth, quarter, dotted quarter, and dotted half notes in this time signature.

Recommended Books to Study Before Beginning the Breval Sonata

- Finger Exercises for Cello, Book One (CHP101)
- Playing in Keys for Cello, Book One (CHP242)
- Cello Stretching: Extended First Position (CHP243)
- Open-String Bow Workouts for Cello, Book One (CHP353)
- Fourth Position for the Cello (CHP131) or Fourth Position Study Method (CHPD078)
- Second Position for the Cello (CHP116)
- The Two Octaves Book for Cello (CHP122)

Movement I Exercises, Part One: The Right Hand

Quarter Note Bowings

Staccato: Stop the Bow Sharply on the String

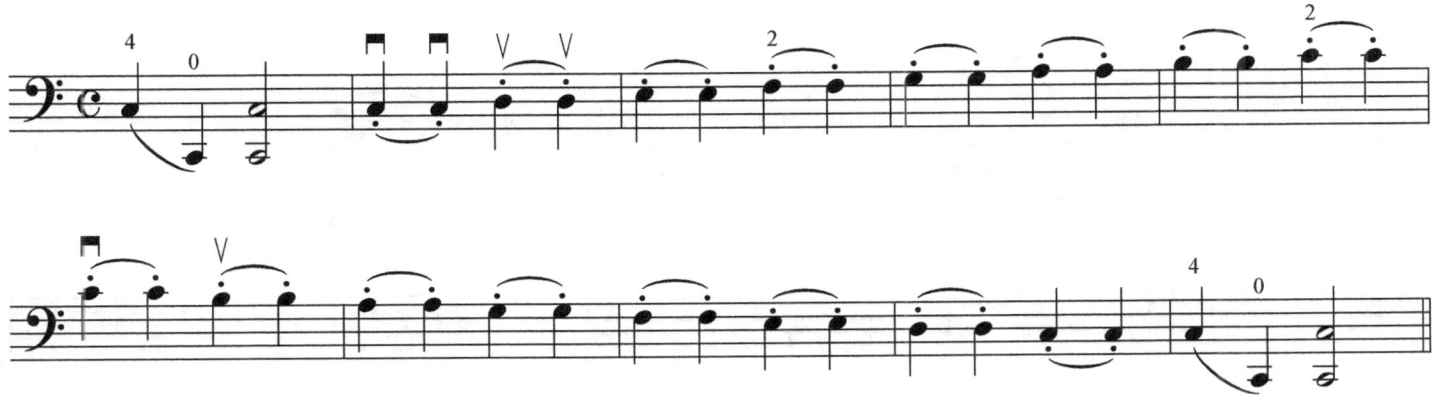

The Breval Sonata in C Major Practice Edition for Cello - Preparatory Exercises for Movement One

Eighth Notes

Preparing for "Fiddle" Bowing

14 The Breval Sonata in C Major Practice Edition for Cello - Preparatory Exercises for Movement One

"Fiddle" Bowing: Measures 13, 42

Rhythm: Measures 12, 16, 41

©2021 C. Harvey Publications All Rights Reserved.

The Breval Sonata in C Major Practice Edition for Cello - Preparatory Exercises for Movement One

Dotted Quarter Notes

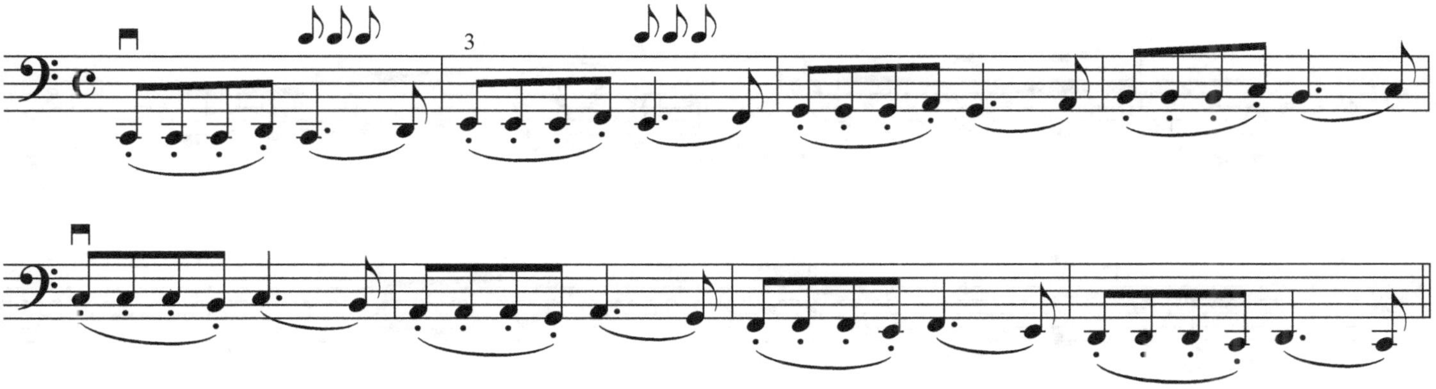

Dotted Quarter Note Variation: Measures 23-24

Dotted Quarter Variation for Bow Speed Changes: Measures 32, 35, 96

16　The Breval Sonata in C Major Practice Edition for Cello - Preparatory Exercises for Movement One

Dotted Quarter Variation No. 1 for Quick Changes: Measures 5, 70

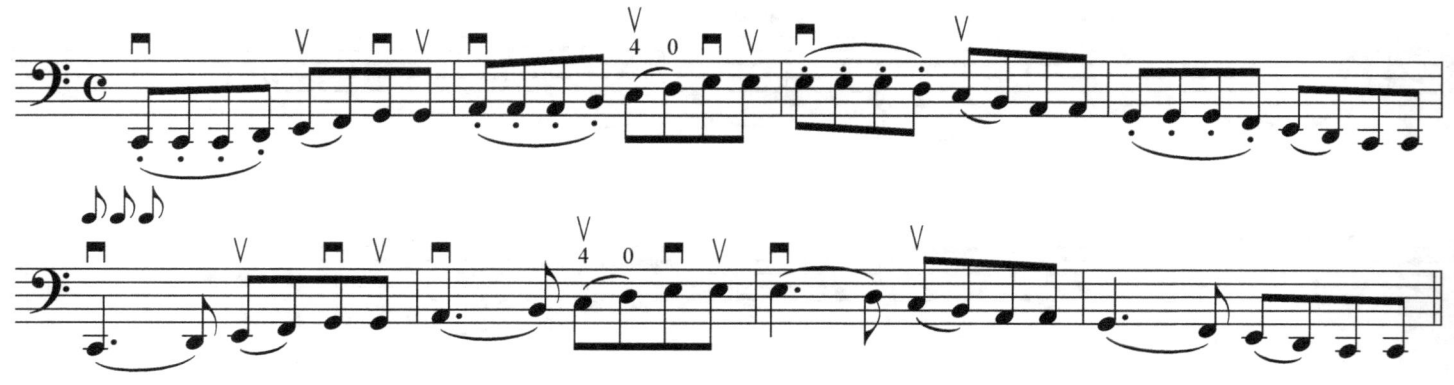

Dotted Quarter Variation No. 2 for Quick Changes: Measures 5, 70

Dotted Quarter Slurs: Bowing No. 1: Measure 53, 55

©2021 C. Harvey Publications All Rights Reserved.

The Breval Sonata in C Major Practice Edition for Cello - Preparatory Exercises for Movement One 17

18 The Breval Sonata in C Major Practice Edition for Cello - Preparatory Exercises for Movement One

C Major Scale in Triplets

Triplet Rhythm Study: Measures 26, 93, 98

©2021 C. Harvey Publications All Rights Reserved.

Uneven Bowing Exercise No. 1

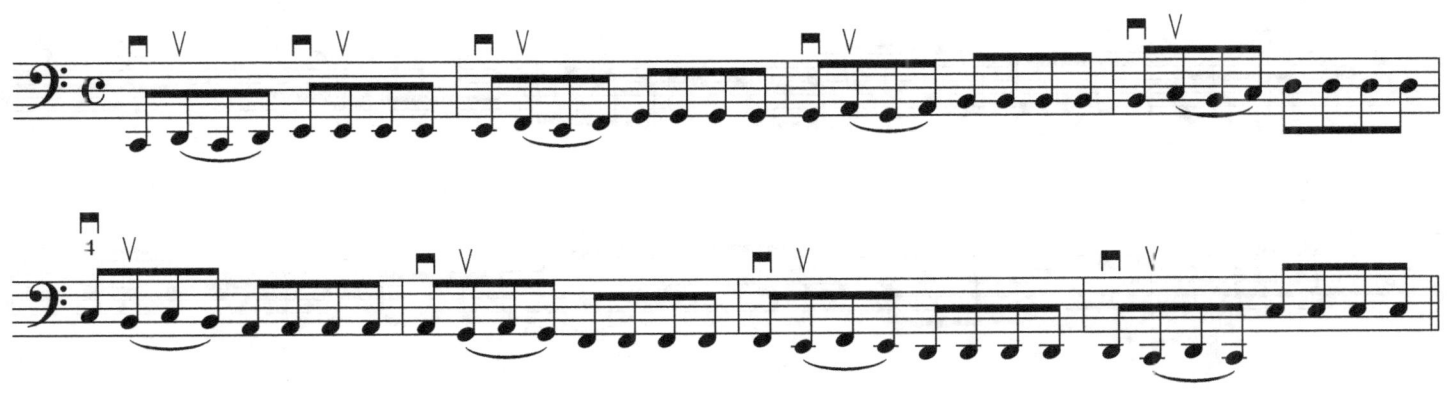

Uneven Bowing Exercise No. 2: Measures 91, 92

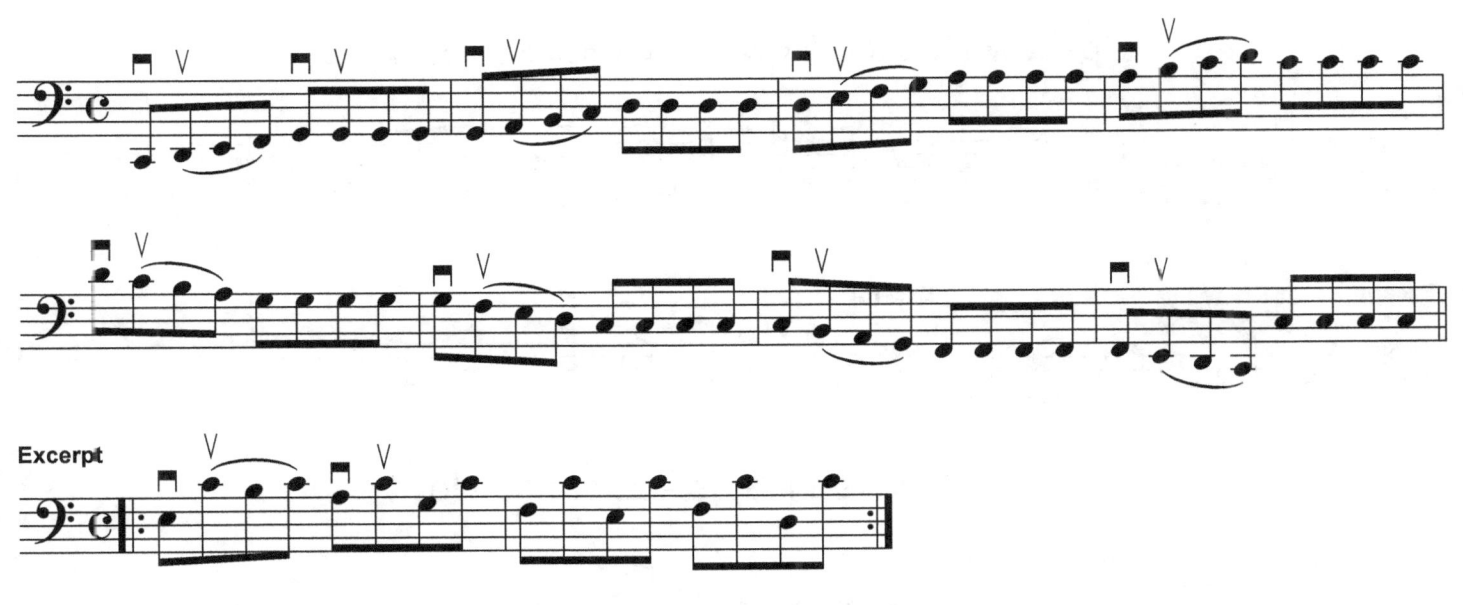

Excerpt

Uneven Bowing Exercise No. 3 (Up-Bow Start)

Start on an up-bow!

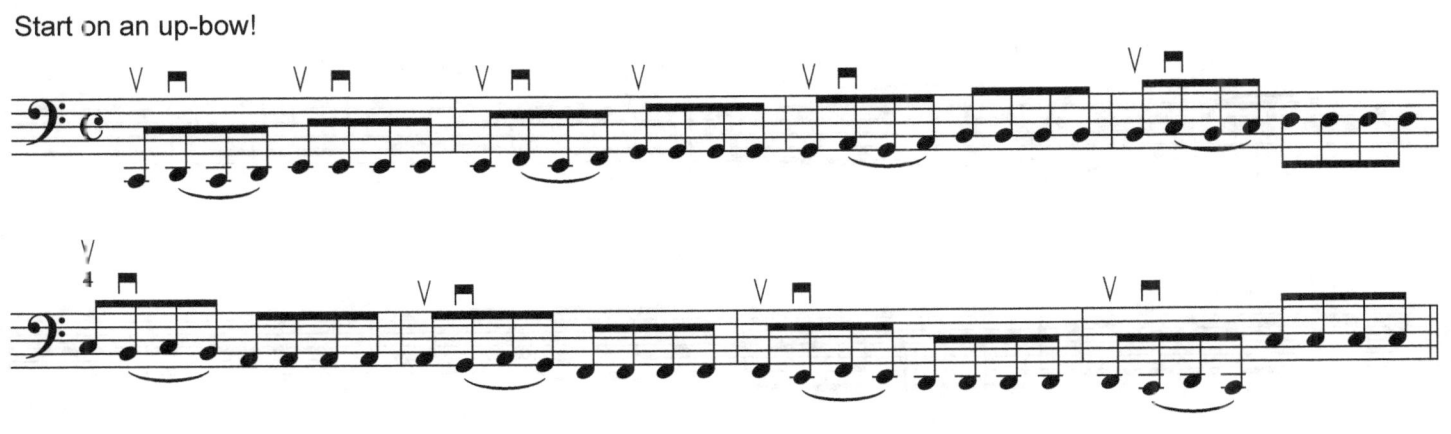

Uneven Bowing Exercise No. 4: Measures 91, 92 (Up-Bow Start)

Start on an up-bow!

Up-Bow Hooked Bowing: Measures 9, 15, 17, etc.

Three Hooked Notes - Exercise No. 1

The Breval Sonata in C Major Practice Edition for Cello - Preparatory Exercises for Movement One

Three Hooked Notes - Exercise No. 6: Measures 56-57

Excerpt

Bow Rhythm with Three Hooked Notes: Measures 7-8, 72-73

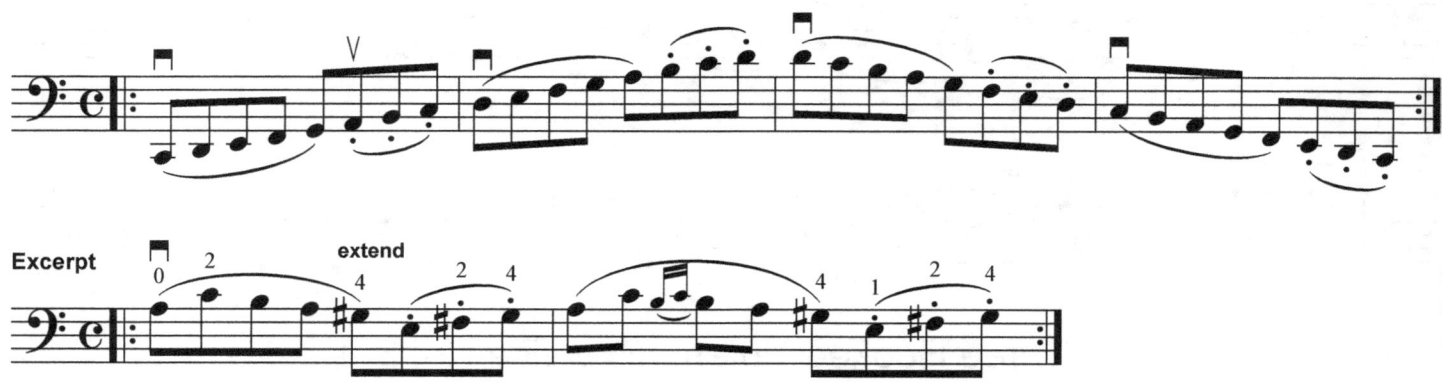

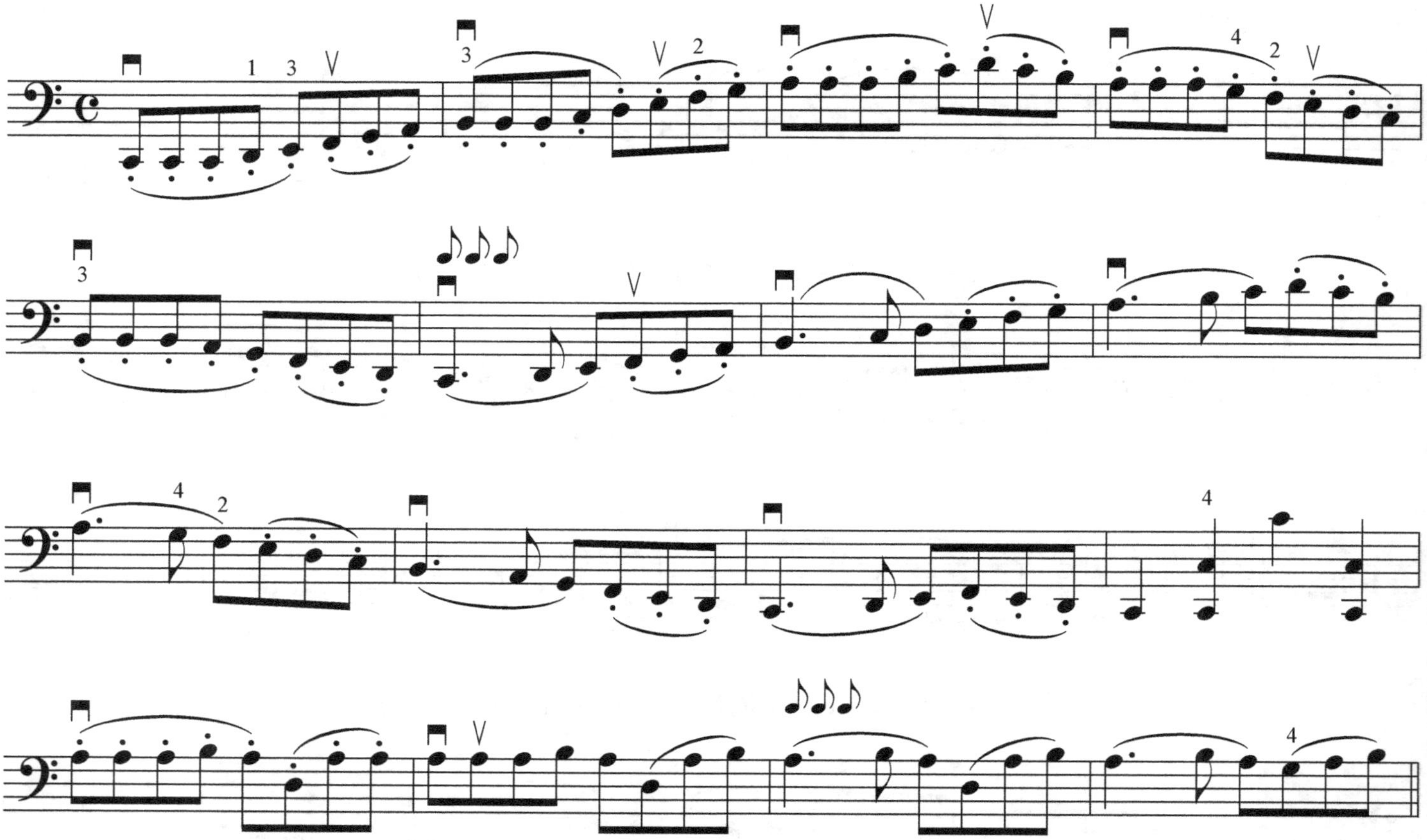

Excerpt

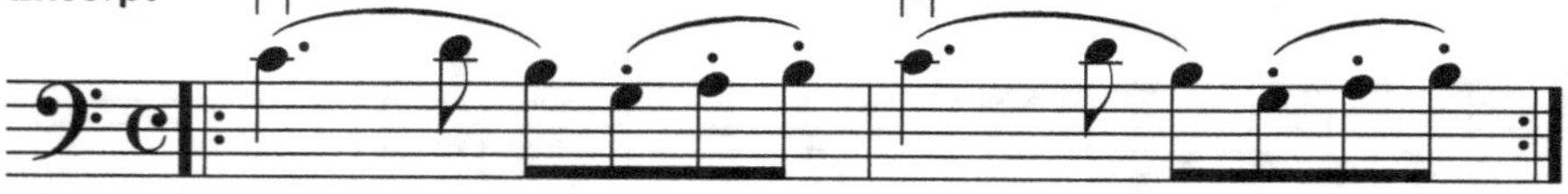

The Breval Sonata in C Major Practice Edition for Cello - Preparatory Exercises for Movement One   23

Slurring Across Bar Lines: Measures 18-20

Note: See page 41 to learn how to play the trills in these measures.

Stopping the Bow Gently: Measures 20-21

Bow Rhythms Before Stopping the Bow Gently: Measures 18-21

Note: See page 44 for excerpts for these measures.

©2021 C. Harvey Publications All Rights Reserved.

The Breval Sonata in C Major Practice Edition for Cello - Preparatory Exercises for Movement One

Learning the Short-Long Rhythm

Short-Long on a Scale: Measure 50

Slurs, Hooked Notes, and Short-Long: Measure 9

©2021 C. Harvey Publications All Rights Reserved.

The Breval Sonata in C Major Practice Edition for Cello - Preparatory Exercises for Movement One

Dotted Quarter and Sixteenths: Measures 14, 43

The Breval Sonata in C Major Practice Edition for Cello - Preparatory Exercises for Movement One

A Tricky Triplet Slur Pattern: Measure 27

Scale Study in Triplets: Measure 27

Putting a Scale Together: Measure 27

Excerpt

©2021 C. Harvey Publications All Rights Reserved.

The Breval Sonata in C Major Practice Edition for Cello - Preparatory Exercises for Movement One

Counting Quarter Notes Tied to Eighth Notes: Measures 58-61

Note: See page 48 for excerpts for these measures.

Subdividing Into Eighth Notes: Measure 64

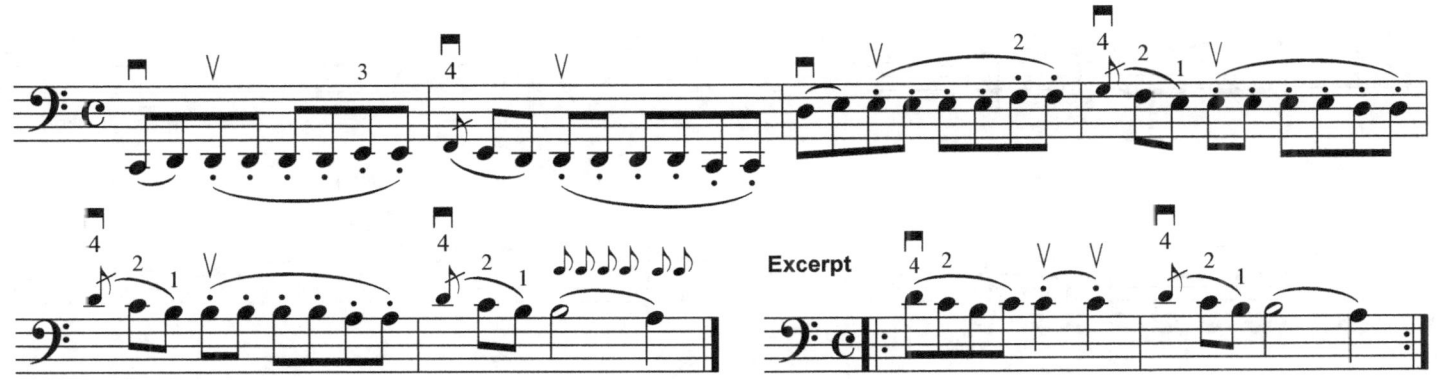

©2021 C. Harvey Publications All Rights Reserved.

Learning the Syncopation: Measures 33, 36

The Breval Sonata in C Major Practice Edition for Cello - Preparatory Exercises for Movement One

Hooked Bowing Into Syncopation: Measures 32-33, 35-36

The Breval Sonata in C Major Practice Edition for Cello - Preparatory Exercises for Movement One

Rhythm, Hooked Bowing, Syncopation: Measures 32-33, 35-36

The Breval Sonata in C Major Practice Edition for Cello - Preparatory Exercises for Movement One

Fitting Dotted Note Combinations Inside One Beat: Exercise No. 1

Fitting Dotted Note Combinations Inside One Beat: Exercise No. 2

Dotted Note Combination Scale

©2021 C. Harvey Publications All Rights Reserved.

Dotted Note Combination Slurred Across Beats
Measures 37-38, 103-104

Movement 1 Exercises, Part Two: The Left Hand
Positions Used in the Breval Sonata

On this page, only whole steps are marked. Any steps not marked are half steps.

First Position Closed

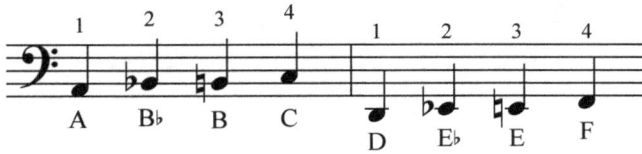

First Position Extended

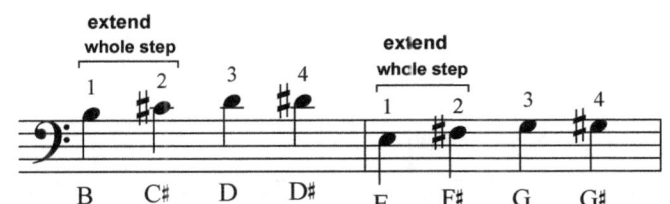

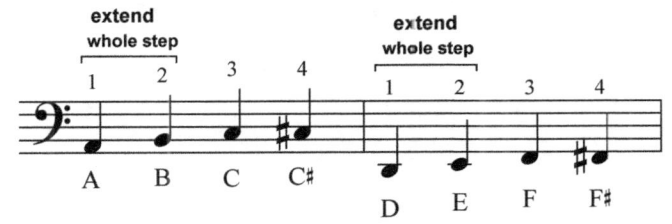

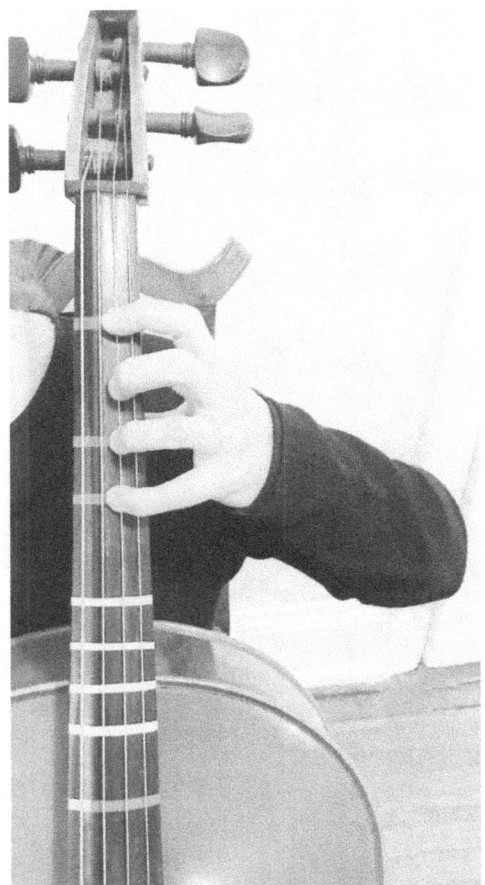

On this page, only whole steps are marked. Any steps not marked are half steps.

Second Position Closed

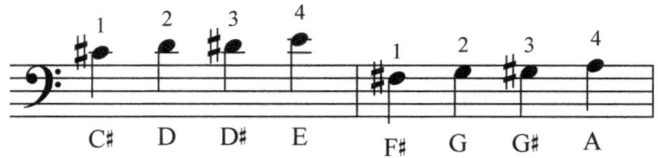

Second Position Extended

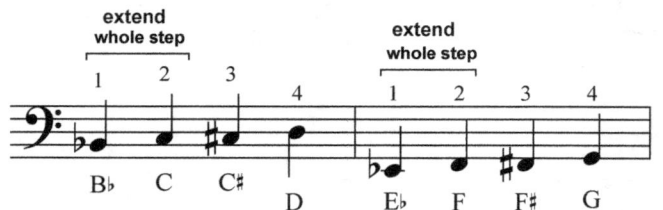

The Breval Sonata in C Major Practice Edition for Cello - Preparatory Exercises for Movement One

On this page, only whole steps are marked. Any steps not marked are half steps.

Third Position Closed

High Third Position Closed

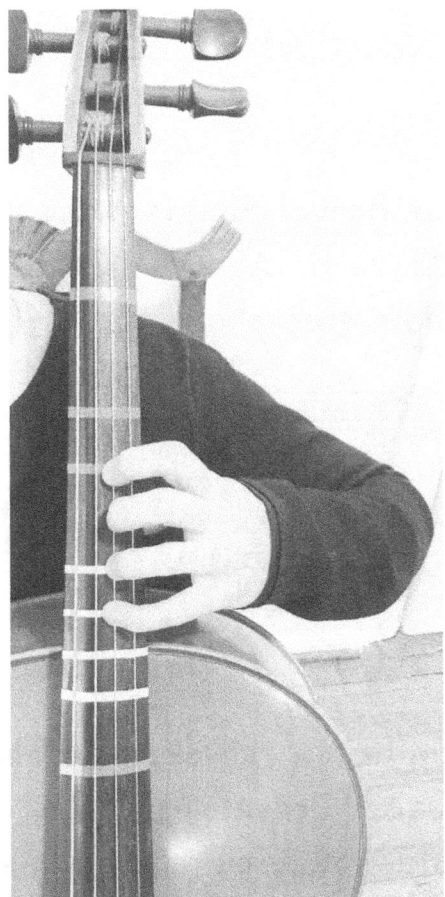

©2021 C. Harvey Publications All Rights Reserved.

On this page, only whole steps are marked. Any steps not marked are half steps.

Fourth Position Closed

About Trills

A trill is an embellishment. To play a trill in the Breval Sonata, play the written note rapidly alternating with the note above it. Always trill to the next note in the scale (this may be a half or whole step above the written note.) The symbol for trill is *tr.*

The trill should continue for the length of the note. In the example above, the trill goes directly into the grace notes. Because Breval originally wrote this as a mordant (single trill), we typically do not play more than one trill in the example above.

The Breval Sonata in C Major Practice Edition for Cello - Preparatory Exercises for Movement One

Movement I Exercises, Part Two: The Left Hand

Switching Fingers Across Strings
Measures 1-2

Building the Chords
Measures 1-2

©2021 C. Harvey Publications All Rights Reserved.

38

The Breval Sonata in C Major Practice Edition for Cello - Preparatory Exercises for Movement One

Chord Work
Measures 1-2

Rhythm
Measures 1-4

Retake bow.

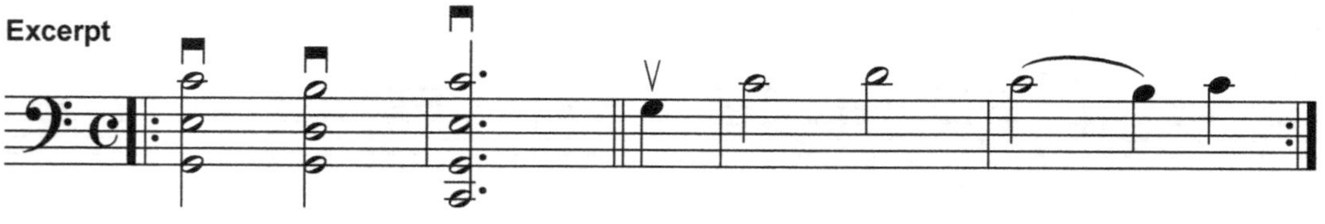

Excerpt

©2021 C. Harvey Publications   All Rights Reserved.

The Breval Sonata in C Major Practice Edition for Cello - Preparatory Exercises for Movement One

Agility Exercise No. 1 for Trills
Measures 6, 19-20, 33, 36, etc.

♩=110-140 (or as fast as you can go)

Repeat this exercise as many times as you wish, playing faster each time.

Agility Exercise No. 2 for Trills

♩=110-140 (or as fast as you can go)

©2021 C. Harvey Publications All Rights Reserved.

Learning Groups of Five Notes

How the "Trill Plus Grace Notes" Can Be Played: Measure 6

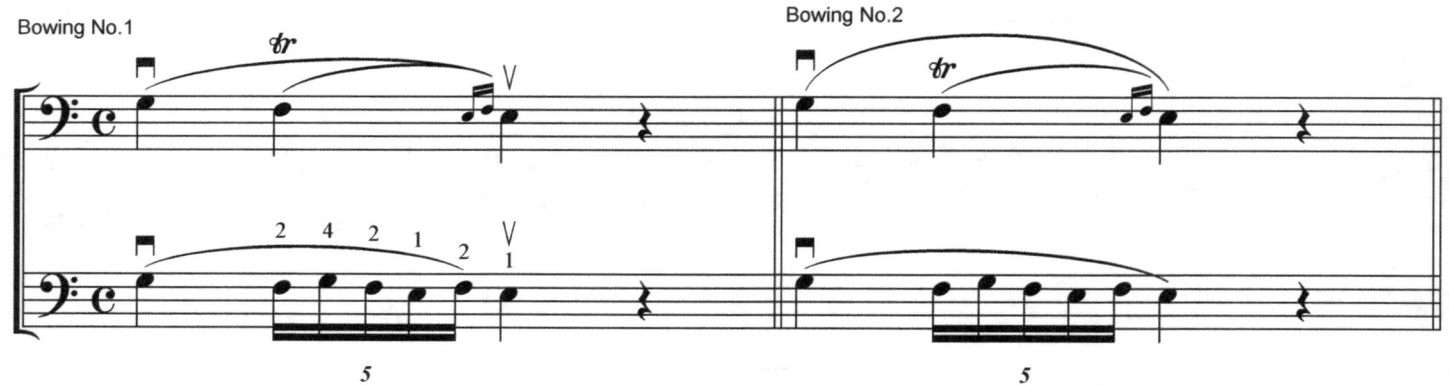

Trill Plus Grace Notes: Measure 6

The Breval Sonata in C Major Practice Edition for Cello - Preparatory Exercises for Movement One 41

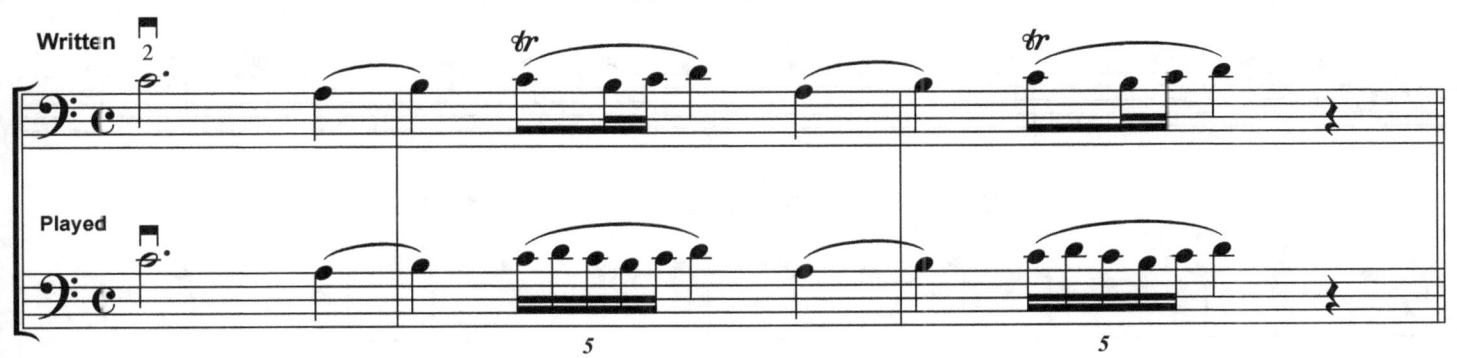

©2021 C. Harvey Publications All Rights Reserved.

42

The Breval Sonata in C Major Practice Edition for Cello - Preparatory Exercises for Movement One

Introduction to Second Position, Extended: Measure 21

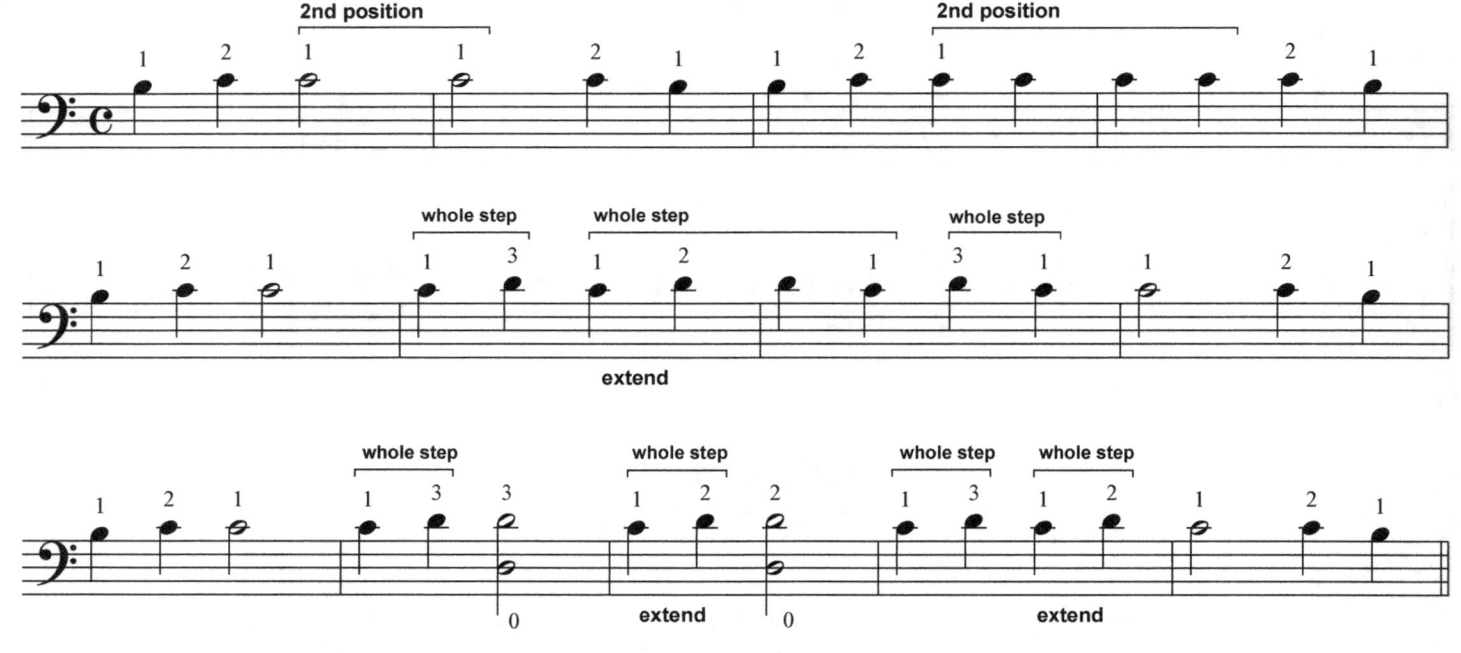

Adding Fourth Finger: Measure 21

©2021 C. Harvey Publications All Rights Reserved.

The Breval Sonata in C Major Practice Edition for Cello - Preparatory Exercises for Movement One

43

Second Position Study No. 1: Measures 20-22

Second Position Study No. 2: Measures 20-22

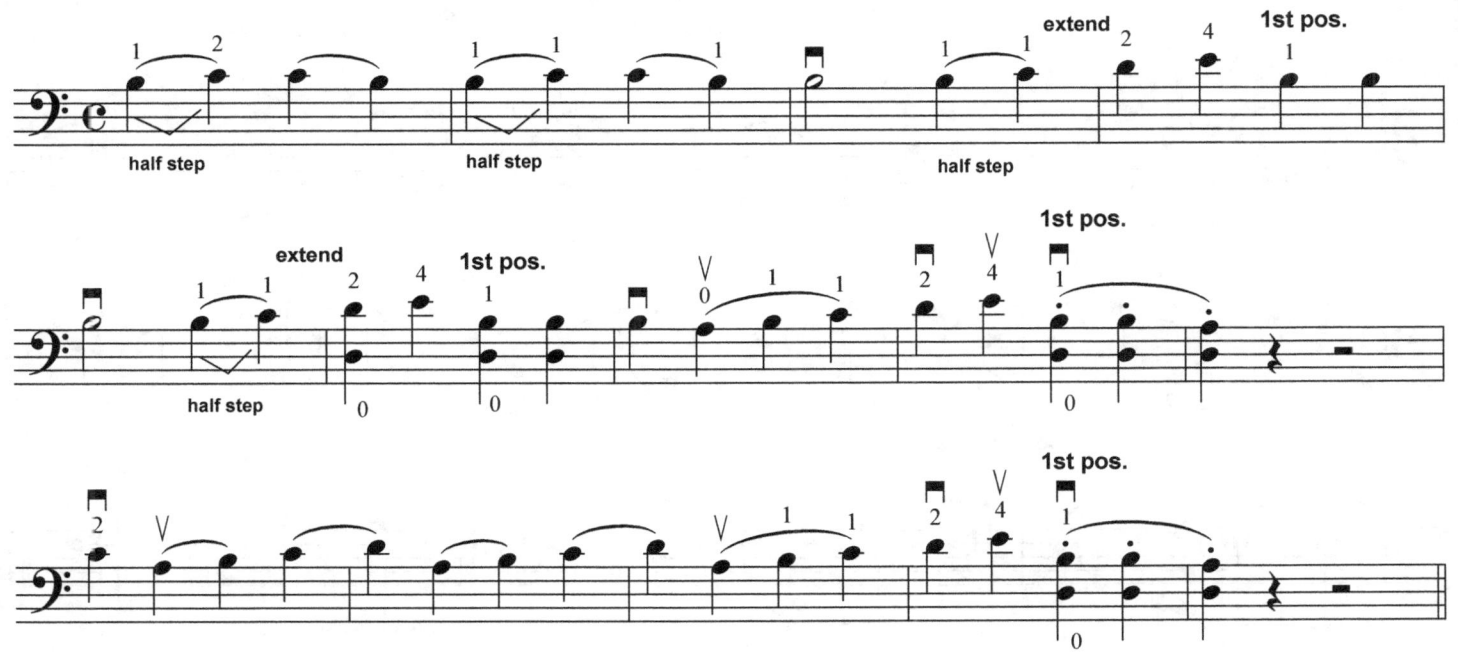

©2021 C. Harvey Publications All Rights Reserved.

44 The Breval Sonata in C Major Practice Edition for Cello - Preparatory Exercises for Movement One

Second Position Study No. 3: Measures 20-22

String Crossing
Measures 29-30

(F♮ to work on 2nd finger agility.)

©2021 C. Harvey Publications All Rights Reserved.

The Breval Sonata in C Major Practice Edition for Cello - Preparatory Exercises for Movement One 45

46 — The Breval Sonata in C Major Practice Edition for Cello - Preparatory Exercises for Movement One

Finding High Third Position: Measures 50-51

Shifting to Third and Fourth Positions
Measures 50-53

©2021 C. Harvey Publications All Rights Reserved.

The Breval Sonata in C Major Practice Edition for Cello - Preparatory Exercises for Movement One

Staccato, Mordant, Extension: Measure 56-57

Shifting to Third Position: Measures 58-59

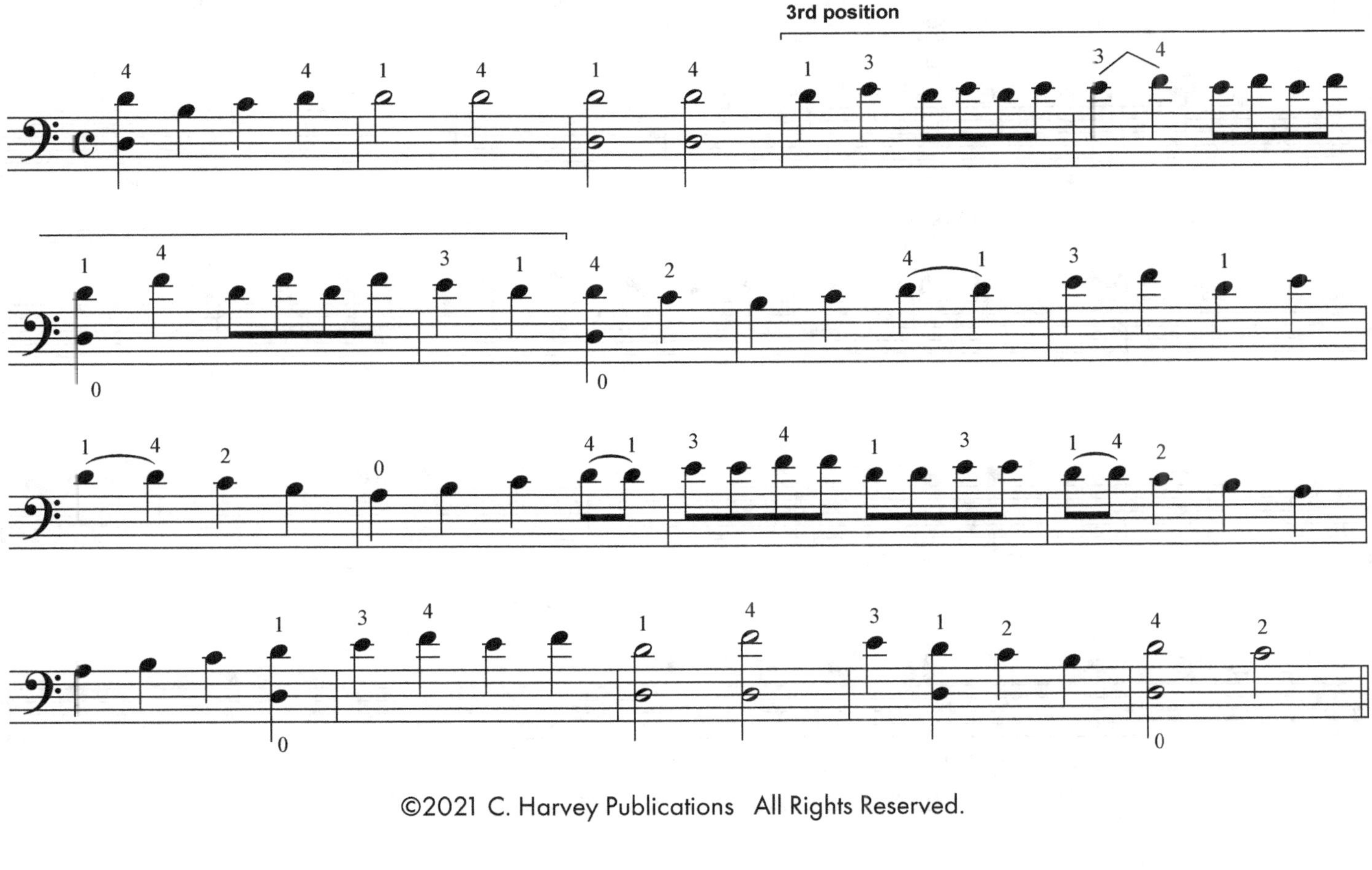

The Breval Sonata in C Major Practice Edition for Cello - Preparatory Exercises for Movement One

Little Scales: Measures 58-59

Learning the Notes: Measures 61-62

©2021 C. Harvey Publications All Rights Reserved.

The Breval Sonata in C Major Practice Edition for Cello - Preparatory Exercises for Movement One

Shifting: Measures 61-62

Little Scales: Measures 60-62

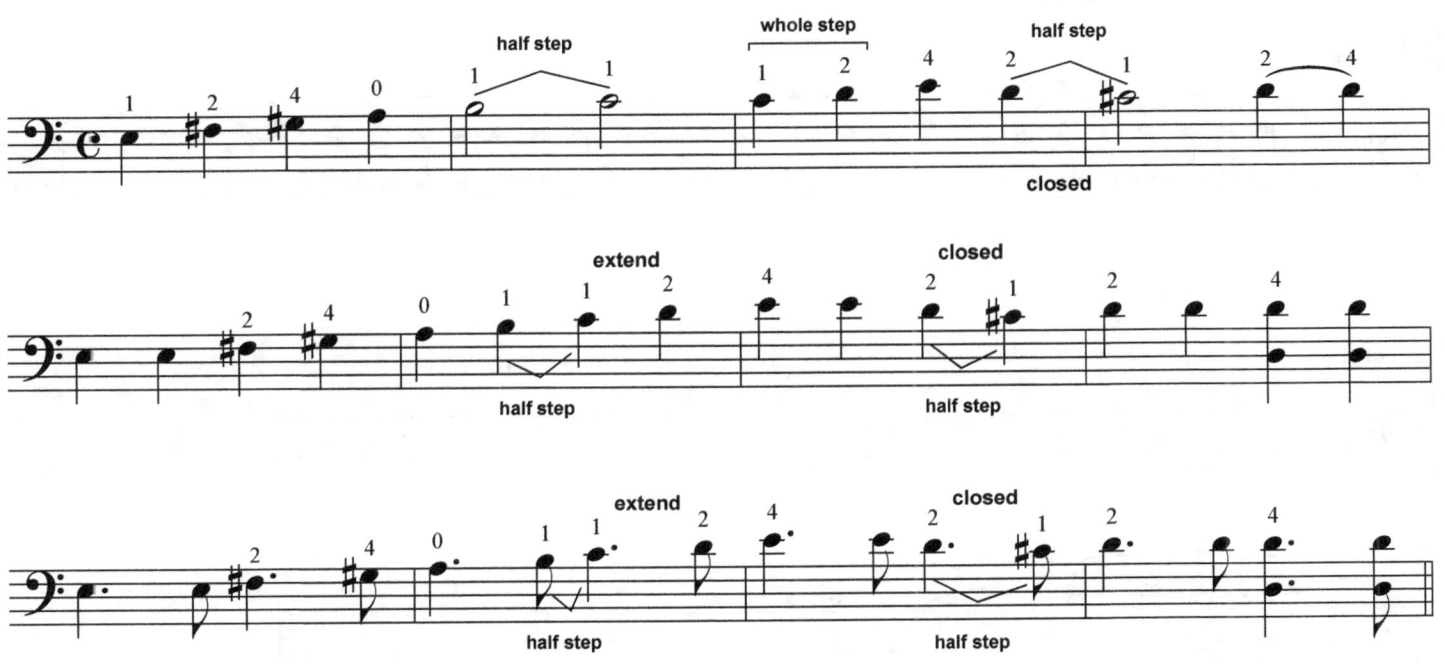

©2021 C. Harvey Publications All Rights Reserved.

Shifting and Extensions: Measures 60-62

Rhythmic Shifting: Measures 60-64

Excerpt

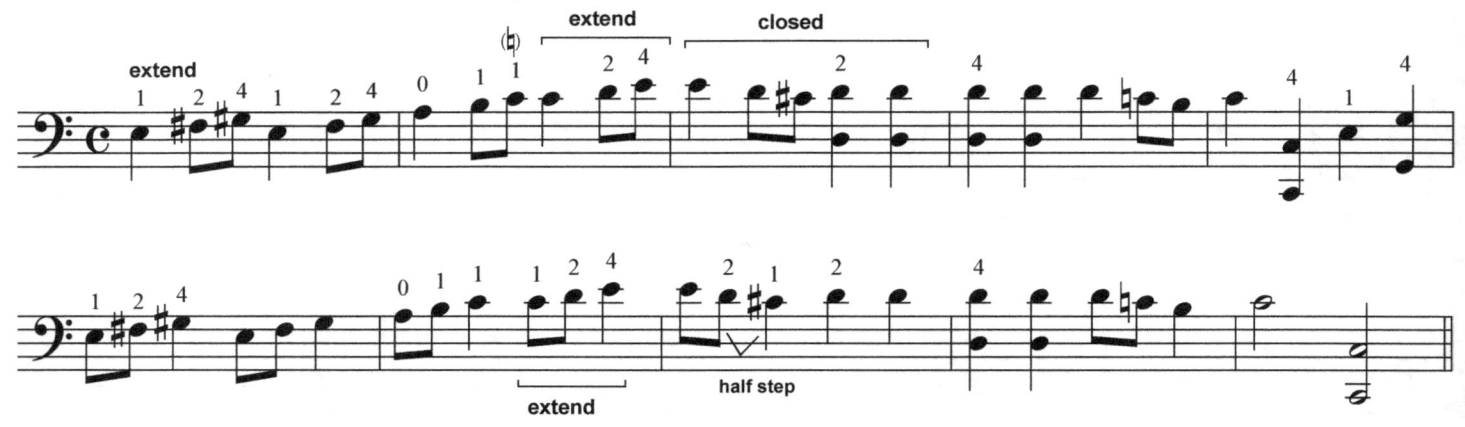

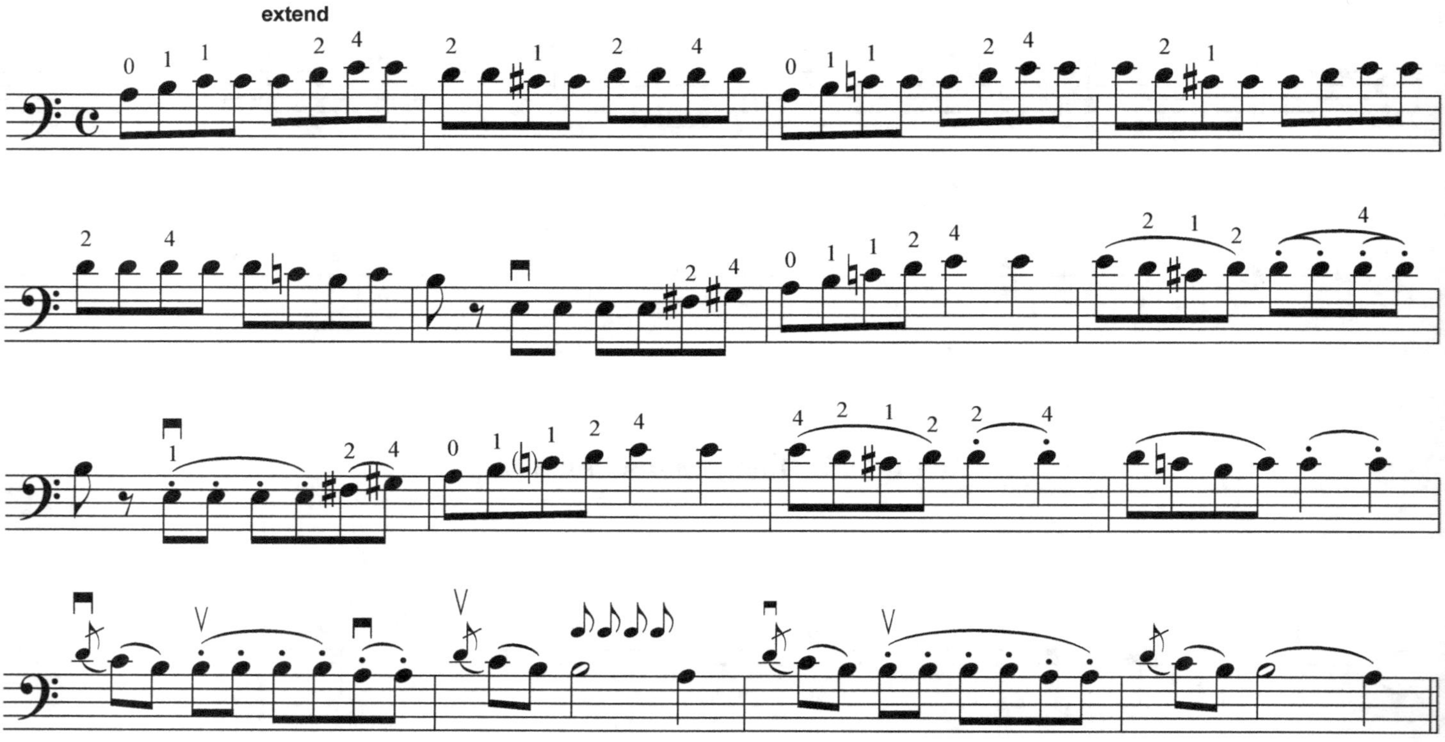

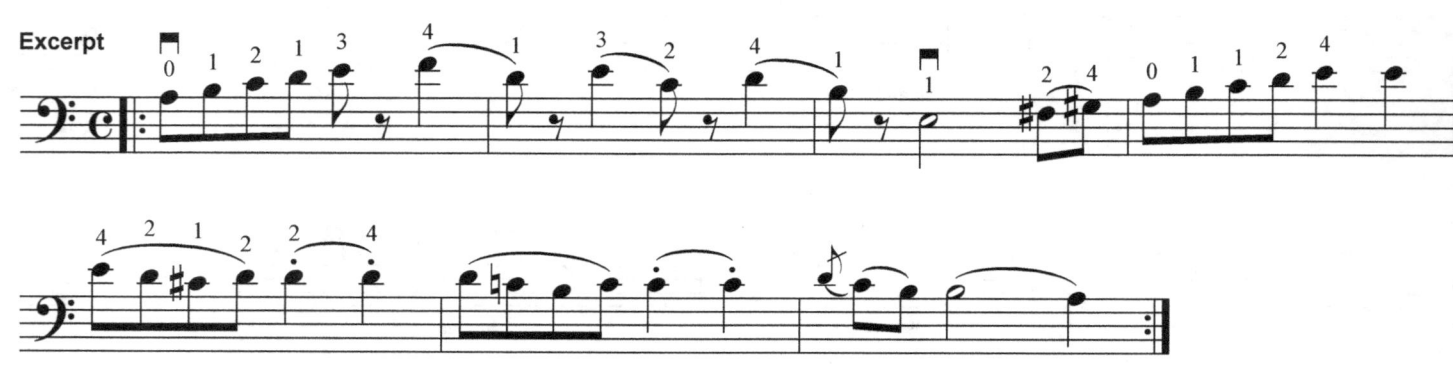

The Breval Sonata in C Major Practice Edition for Cello - Preparatory Exercises for Movement One

Rhythm and String Crossing
Measures 86-90

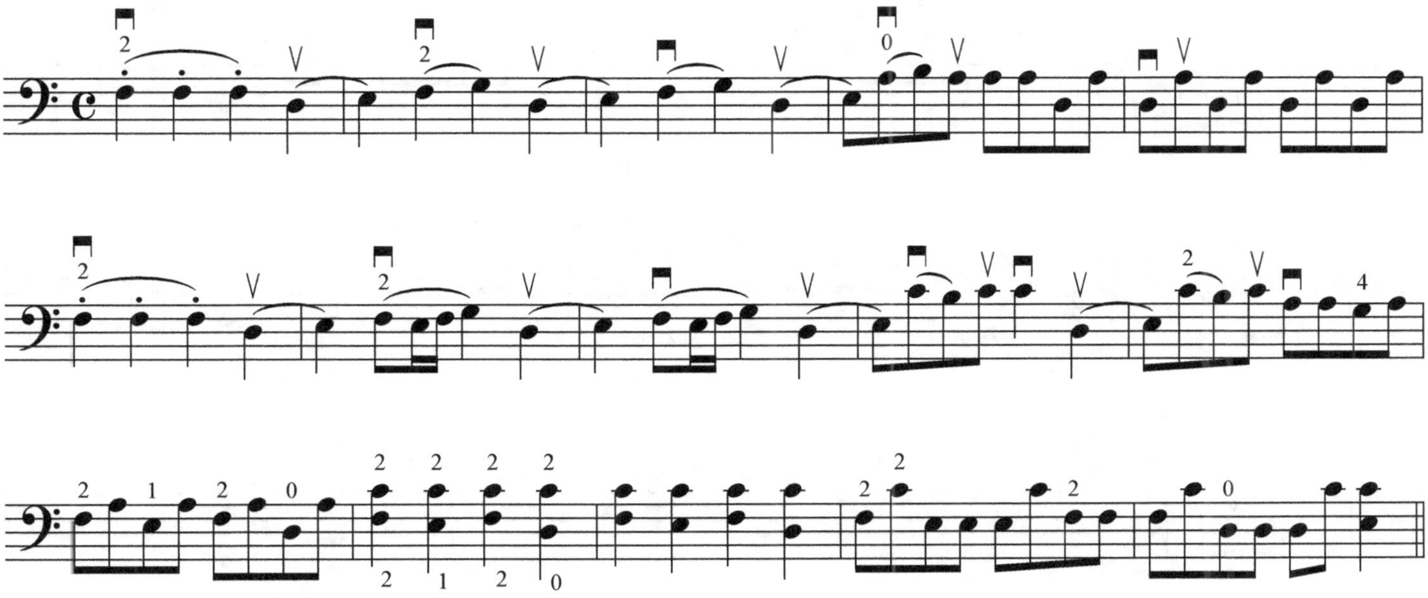

Extended Second Position
Measures 101-102

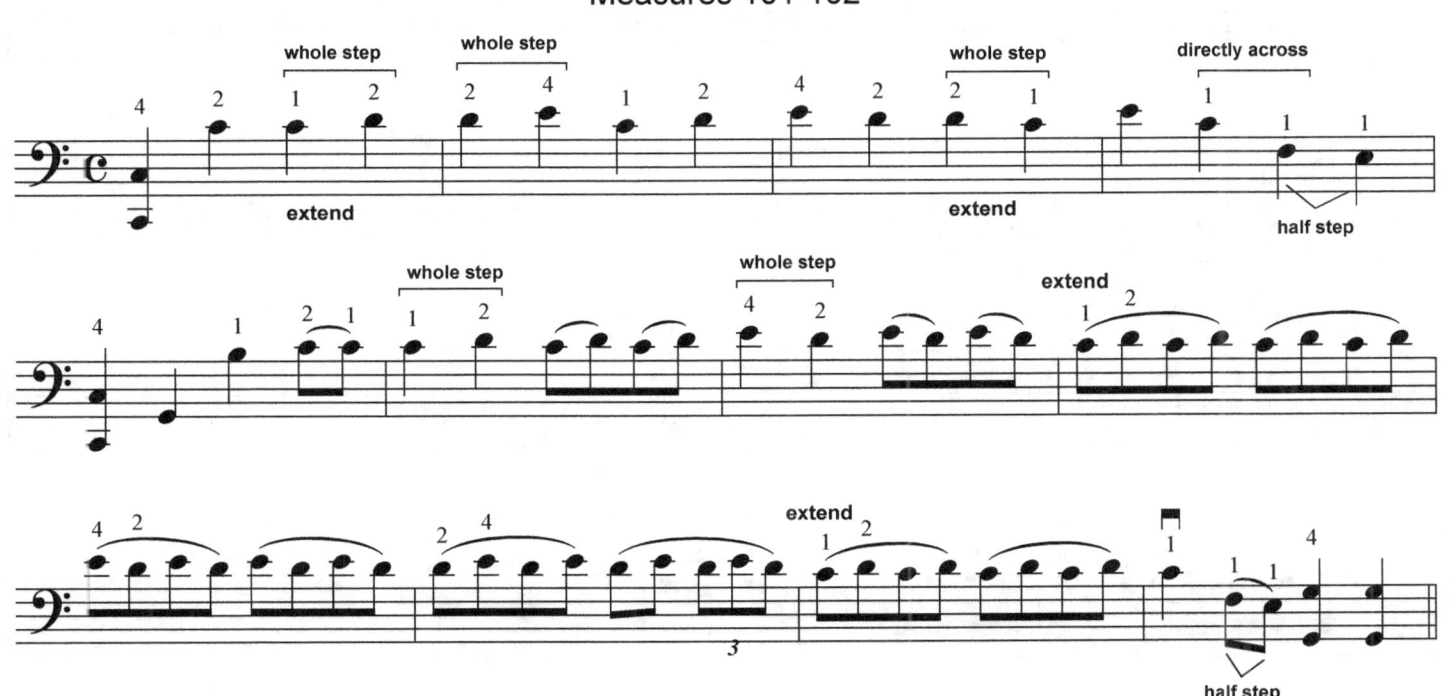

©2021 C. Harvey Publications All Rights Reserved.

52　The Breval Sonata in C Major Practice Edition for Cello - Preparatory Exercises for Movement One

Learning to Shift Quickly: Measures 100-103

Adding the Trill: Measures 101-103

Keep trilling until grace notes at end of measure.

©2021 C. Harvey Publications All Rights Reserved.

The Breval Sonata in C Major Practice Edition for Cello - Preparatory Exercises for Movement One

©2021 C. Harvey Publications All Rights Reserved.

This page is left blank for page turns.

What to Focus on in Movement One

- Play with long bows and a bold, strong tone.

- Play with curved fingers so that the string is stopped completely; this will give you the clearest sound.

- Focus on rhythm and counting correctly. Some measures are easier to learn when you count the eighth note beats (also called *subdividing*.)

- Make sure the difference between eighth notes (2 to a beat) and triplets (3 to a beat) is clear, especially in measures 30-31 and 34-35.

- Make sure you are following the bowings correctly even when it is awkward.

Tempos for Movement One

Start by playing slowly. You may want to set the metronome to an eighth note beat for some of the measures, although this will not work well in the measures with triplets. As you get more confident and your intonation is secure, you may increase the tempo.

The tempos below are only suggestions. Feel free to adjust them to suit your playing!

Suggested Practice Tempo range: ♩=70-84

Suggested Performance Tempo range: ♩=86-114

56

The Breval Sonata in C Major Practice Edition for Cello - Movement One With Study Notes

Movement One with Study Notes

I = A string
II = D string
III = G string
IV = C string

J. Breval
Arr. C. Schroeder
Edited C. Harvey

©2021 C. Harvey Publications All Rights Reserved.

The Breval Sonata in C Major Practice Edition for Cello - Movement One With Study Notes 57

©2021 C. Harvey Publications   All Rights Reserved.

58 — The Breval Sonata in C Major Practice Edition for Cello - Movement One With Study Notes

©2021 C. Harvey Publications All Rights Reserved.

The Breval Sonata in C Major Practice Edition for Cello - Movement One With Study Notes

Movement II Exercises, Part One: The Right Hand

Basic Bowings

Staccato: Stop the Bow Sharply on the String

The Breval Sonata in C Major Practice Edition for Cello - Preparatory Exercises for Movement Two

Using Staccato to Establish Rhythm

Rhythm Inside Slurs

Slurs and Light Staccato: Measure 98

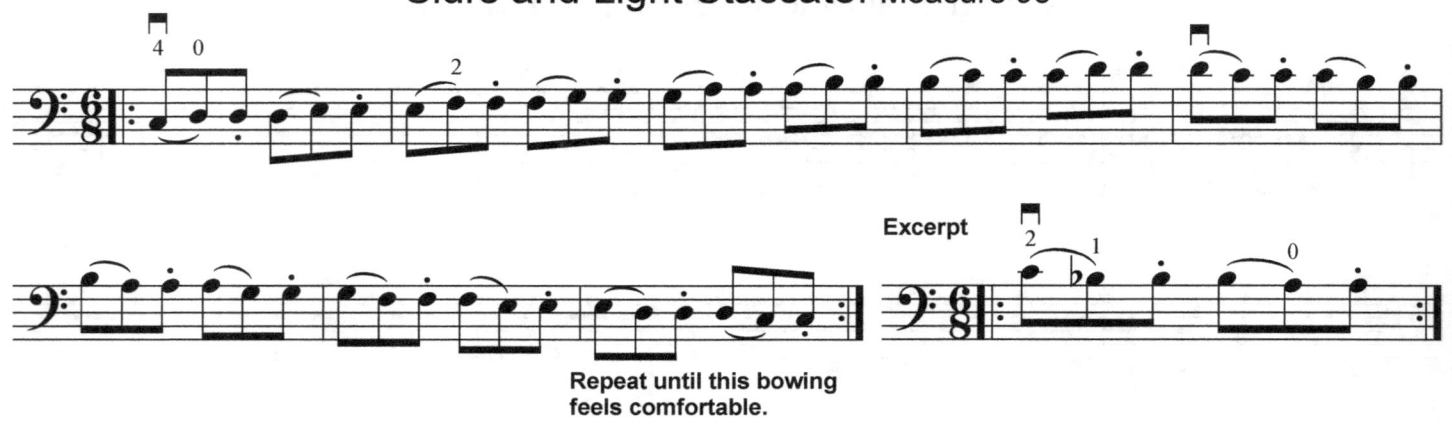

Repeat until this bowing feels comfortable.

Grace Note Variation No. 1: Measures 1, 5, etc.

Grace Note Variation No. 2: Measures 1, 5, etc.

The Breval Sonata in C Major Practice Edition for Cello - Preparatory Exercises for Movement Two

Hooked Bowing
Measures 12-13, and 20-21

Hooked Note Grace Note Combination
Measures 7-8

The Breval Sonata in C Major Practice Edition for Cello - Preparatory Exercises for Movement Two

Counting Tied Notes
Measures 2, 19

Sixteenth Note Triplets: Measures 4, 114

The Bréval Sonata in C Major Practice Edition for Cello - Preparatory Exercises for Movement Two
67

Holding a Tied Note: Measures 74-76

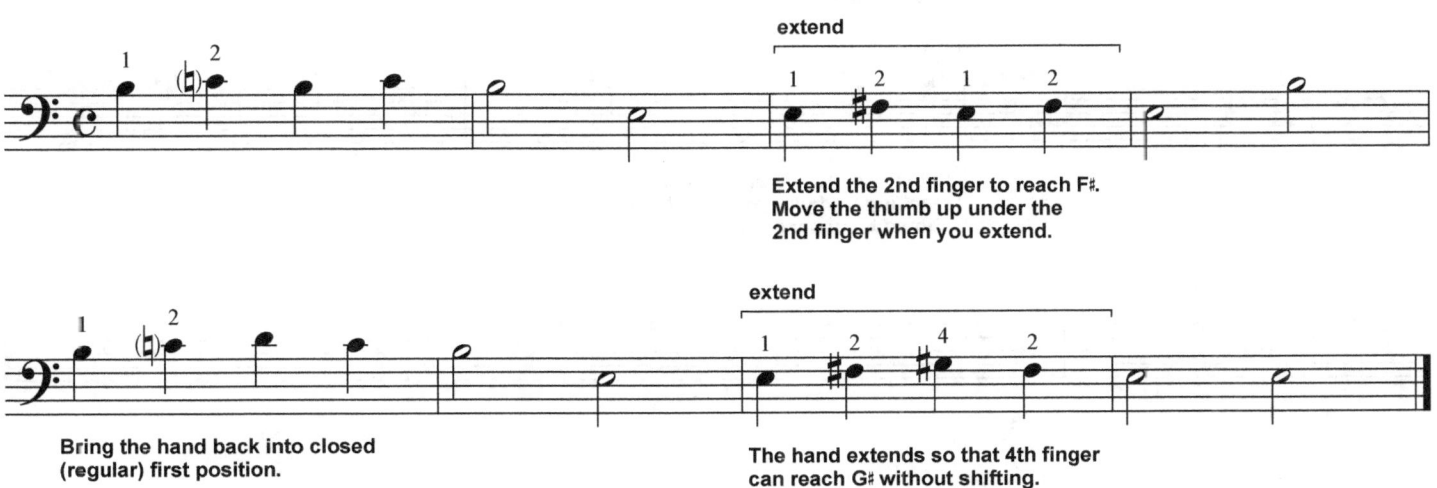

Introduction to Forward Extension: Measure 76

Extend the 2nd finger to reach F♯.
Move the thumb up under the
2nd finger when you extend.

Bring the hand back into closed
(regular) first position.

The hand extends so that 4th finger
can reach G♯ without shifting.

©2021 C. Harvey Publications All Rights Reserved.

The Breval Sonata in C Major Practice Edition for Cello - Preparatory Exercises for Movement Two

Running Sixteenth Notes: Measures 95-97

Extending Back in a Scale Pattern: Measures 95-97

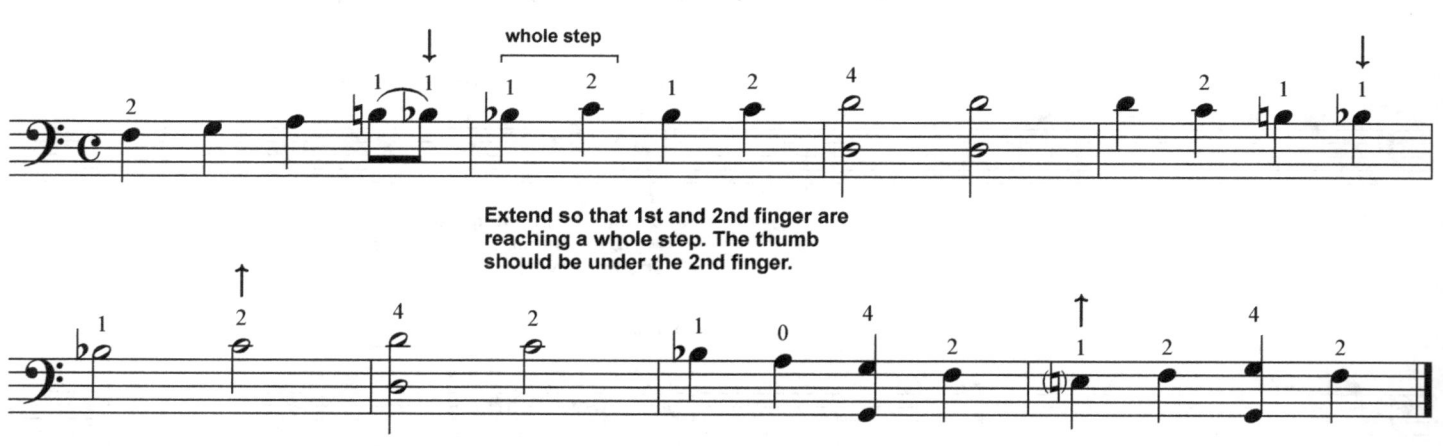

Extend so that 1st and 2nd finger are reaching a whole step. The thumb should be under the 2nd finger.

Excerpt

©2021 C. Harvey Publications All Rights Reserved.

The Breval Sonata in C Major Practice Edition for Cello - Preparatory Exercises for Movement Two

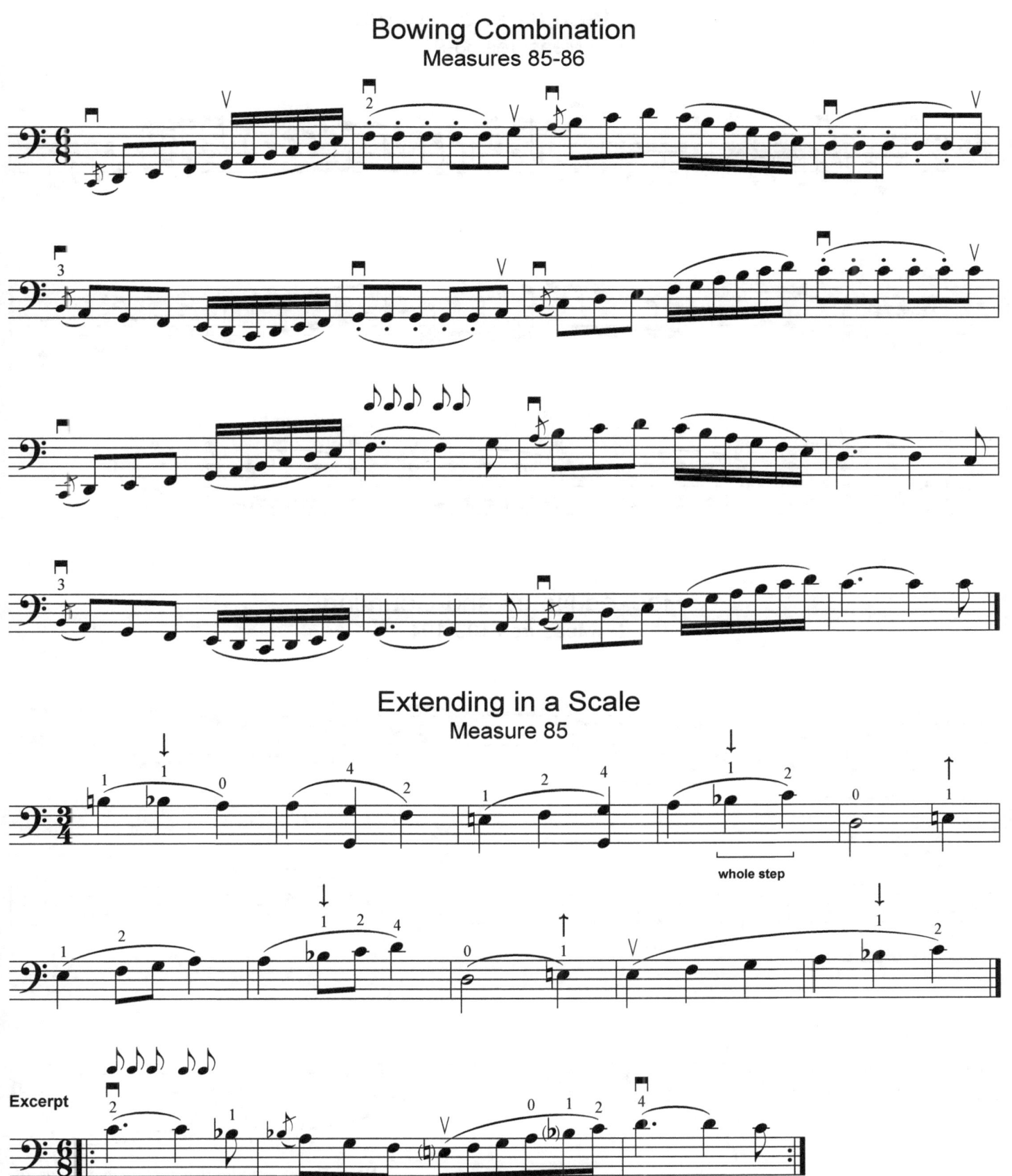

Sixteenths and Eighths
Measures 88-91

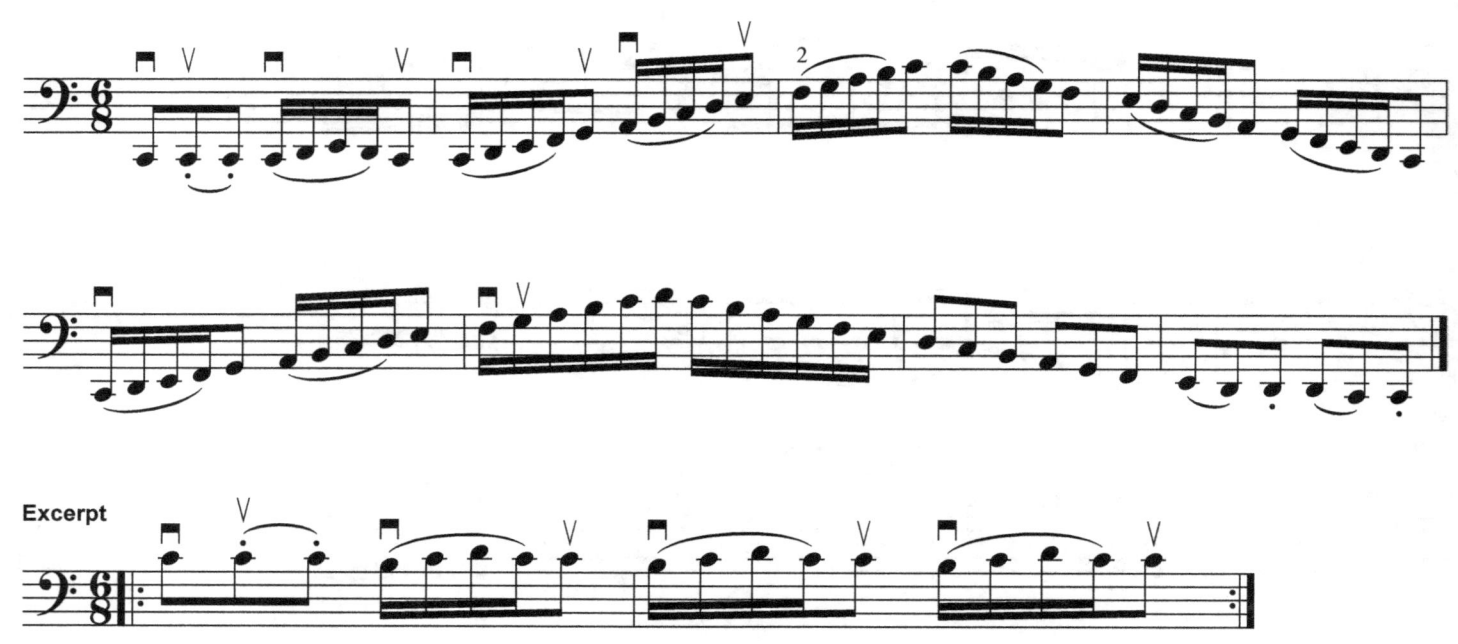

Hooked Notes and Counting
Measures 103-104

Note: The excerpt for this section in on page 76.

The Breval Sonata in C Major Practice Edition for Cello - Preparatory Exercises for Movement Two

Movement II Exercises, Part Two: The Left Hand

Finger Exercise: Measures 27, 33

©2021 C. Harvey Publications All Rights Reserved.

The Breval Sonata in C Major Practice Edition for Cello - Preparatory Exercises for Movement Two

Trill and Grace Notes: Measures 32, 38, 94, 100

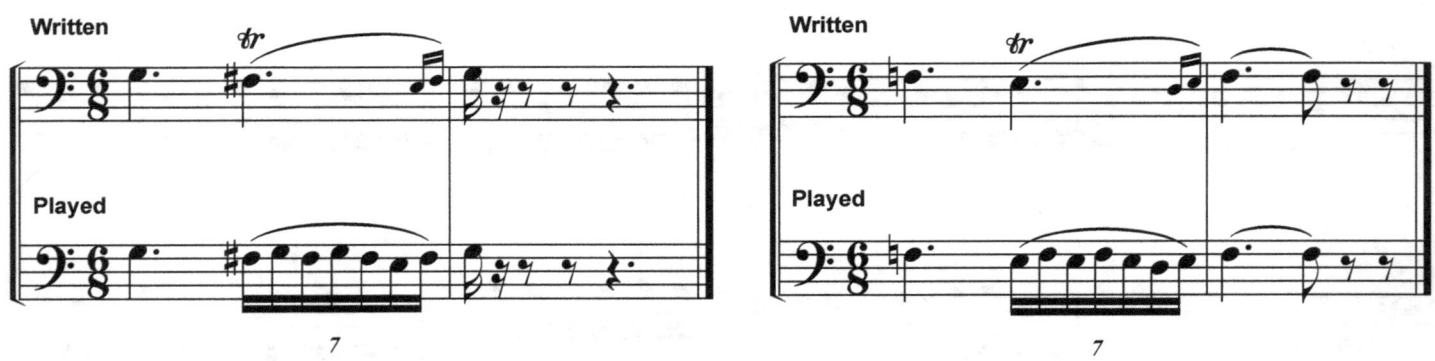

Closed Second Position: Measure 50

©2021 C. Harvey Publications   All Rights Reserved.

The Breval Sonata in C Major Practice Edition for Cello - Preparatory Exercises for Movement Two

Don't forget:
II means D string!

Fourth Position: Measures 66-68

Extended Second Position: Measures 69-71

©2021 C. Harvey Publications   All Rights Reserved.

Extended Second Position and Rhythm: Measures 69-71

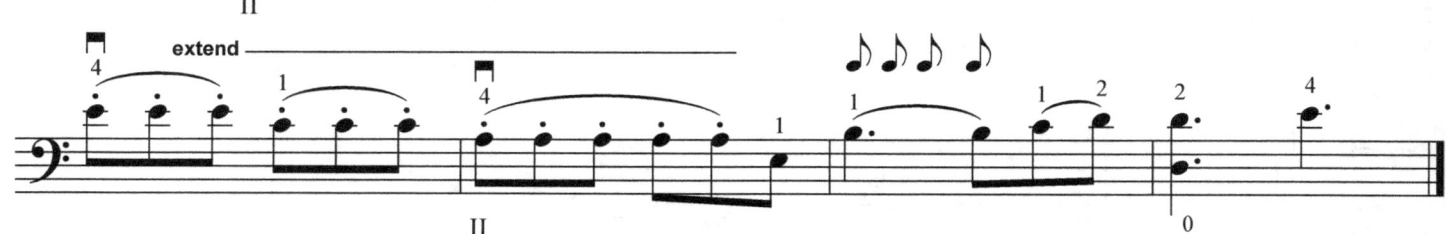

Excerpt

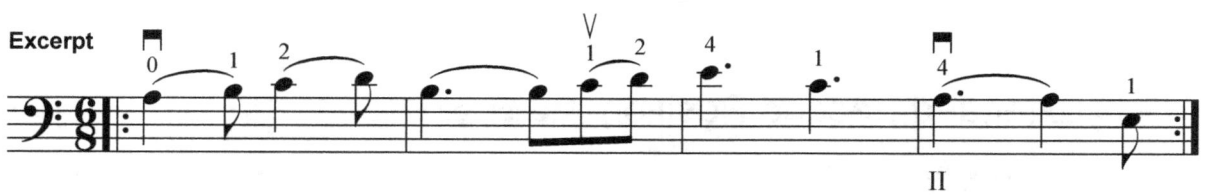

Closed Second Position: Measures 74-75

Excerpt

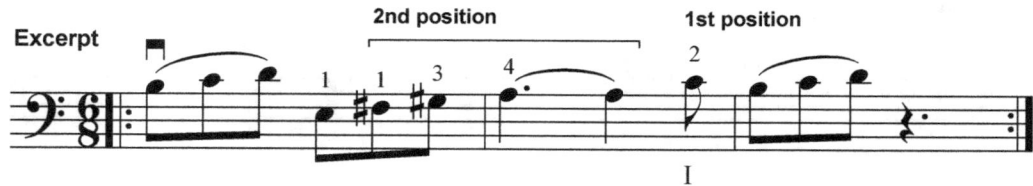

The Brēval Sonata in C Major Practice Edition for Cello - Preparatory Exercises for Movement Two

Extension Practice: Measures 76-77

Extension in a Scale Pattern: Measure 90

The Breval Sonata in C Major Practice Edition for Cello - Preparatory Exercises for Movement Two

Shifting, Extending, and then Closing I: Measures 107-110

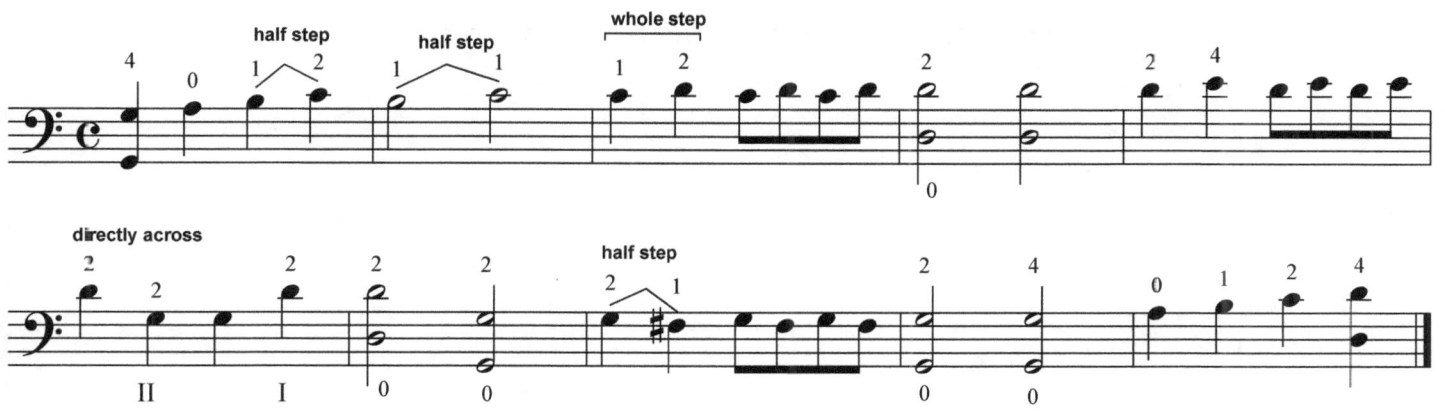

Shifting, Extending, and then Closing II: Measures 107-110

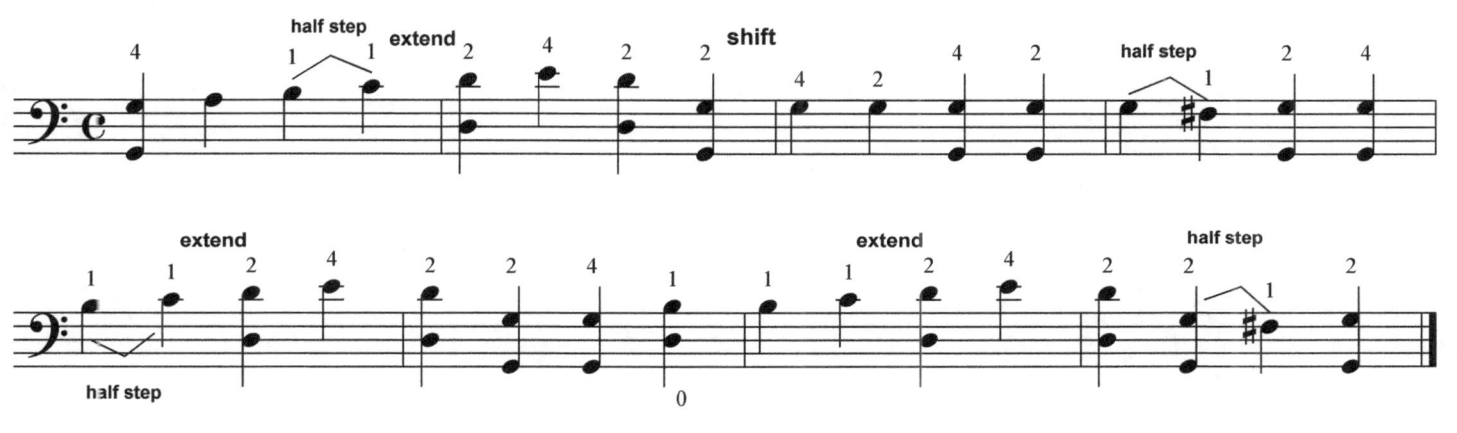

Shifting in Rhythm: Measures 109-110

©2021 C. Harvey Publications All Rights Reserved.

This page is left blank for page turns.

What to Focus on in Movement Two

- Play with clearly articulated fingers and bow; no "mushy" sounds. Playing with curved fingers so that the string is stopped completely will give you the clearest sound.

- The overall style of this movement is light and cheerful but make sure your softer (mp or p) sections are still able to be clearly heard. Keep the bow straight and make sure the bow connects with the string and makes it ring. No matter how loud or soft the music is supposed to be, the string still needs to vibrate.

- Focus on rhythm and counting correctly. In this movement, switching from eighth notes to quarter or dotted quarter notes can be tricky. Be careful to count these measures very carefully and slow your bow speed down on the slower notes.

- Count tied notes very carefully. Sub-divide into eighth notes to make sure you are holding the notes long enough.

- Don't take any extra time for the grace notes. The grace notes fall slightly before the regular note because grace notes are embellishments; not the melody. The regular note needs to fall exactly on the beat.

Tempos for Movement Two

Start by playing slowly. The tempos below are only suggestions. Feel free to adjust them to suit your playing!

Suggested Practice Tempo range: ♪=120-144 or ♩.=40-48

Suggested Performance Tempo range: ♪=156-180 or ♩.=52-60

80

The Breval Sonata in C Major Practice Edition for Cello - Movement Two With Study Notes

Movement Two with Study Notes

©2021 C. Harvey Publications All Rights Reserved.

The Breval Sonata in C Major Practice Edition for Cello - Movement Two With Study Notes   81

©2021 C. Harvey Publications All Rights Reserved.

82

The Breval Sonata in C Major Practice Edition for Cello - Movement Two With Study Notes

©2021 C. Harvey Publications All Rights Reserved.

The Bréval Sonata in C Major Practice Edition for Cello - Movement Two With Study Notes
83

Movement One

J. Breval
Arr. C. Schroeder
Edited C. Harvey

The Breval Sonata in C Major Practice Edition for Cello - Complete Piece, Movement One

Movement Two

The Breval Sonata in C Major Practice Edition for Cello - Complete Piece, Movement Two 87

Sonata

J. Breval
based on an edited version by C. Schroeder

Allegro

The Breval Sonata in C Major Practice Edition for Cello - Duet (Schroader edition) Movement One 89

©2021 C. Harvey Publications All Rights Reserved.

90 — The Breval Sonata in C Major Practice Edition for Cello - Duet (Schroader edition) Movement One

©2021 C. Harvey Publications All Rights Reserved.

The Breval Sonata in C Major Practice Edition for Cello - Duet (Schroader edition) Movement One

©2021 C. Harvey Publications   All Rights Reserved.

The Breval Sonata in C Major Practice Edition for Cello - Duet (Schroader edittion) Movement Two

Rondo grazioso

©2021 C. Harvey Publications All Rights Reserved.

The Breval Sonata in C Major Practice Edition for Cello - Duet (Schroader edittion) Movement Two 93

©2021 C. Harvey Publications   All Rights Reserved.

94 The Breval Sonata in C Major Practice Edition for Cello - Duet (Schroader edittion) Movement Two

©2021 C. Harvey Publications   All Rights Reserved.

The Breval Sonata in C Major Practice Edition for Cello - Duet (Schroader edition) Movement Two
95

Sonata in C Major

J. Breval
Arranged by C. Schroeder
Edited by C. Harvey

©2021 C. Harvey Publications   All Rights Reserved.

The Breval Sonata in C Major Practice Edition for Cello - Piano Accompaniment, Movement One

97

©2021 C. Harvey Publications All Rights Reserved.

98

The Breval Sonata in C Major Practice Edition for Cello - Piano Accompaniment, Movement One

The Breval Sonata in C Major Practice Edition for Cello - Piano Accompaniment, Movement Two

101

©2021 C. Harvey Publications All Rights Reserved.

The Breval Sonata in C Major Practice Edition for Cello - Piano Accompaniment, Movement Two

Sonata

J. Breval

The Breval Sonata in C Major Practice Edition for Cello - Duet from Original Manuscript, Movement One

©2021 C. Harvey Publications All Rights Reserved.

106 The Breval Sonata in C Major Practice Edition for Cello - Duet from Original Manuscript, Movement One

©2021 C. Harvey Publications All Rights Reserved.

The Breval Sonata in C Major Practice Edition for Cello - Duet from Original Manuscript, Movement One

The Breval Sonata in C Major Practice Edition for Cello - Duet from Original Manuscript, Movement Two

The Breval Sonata in C Major Practice Edition for Cello - Duet from Original Manuscript, Movement Two

110
The Breval Sonata in C Major Practice Edition for Cello - Duet from Original Manuscript, Movement Two

©2021 C. Harvey Publications   All Rights Reserved.

The Breval Sonata in C Major Practice Edition for Cello - Duet from Original Manuscript, Movement Two

Cello Curriculum Segments
When to Use the Breval Sonata in a Course of Study

Step One

Methods
- Learning the Cello, Books One (CHP282) and Two (CHP287)
- String Builder, Book One (published Belwin)
- Essential Elements for Cello, Book One (published Hal Leonard)
- Suzuki Book One (if using a modified Suzuki approach) (published Summy-Birchard)

Exercises
- The Open-String Book for Cello (CHP182)
- Early Exercises for Cello (CHP183)
- Beginning Technique for Cello (CHP110)
- Double Stop Beginnings for Cello (CHP220)
- First Position Scale Studies for the Cello (CHP179)
- Playing in Keys for Cello (CHP242)
- Cello Stretching; Extended First Position (CHP243)

Supplements
- Cello Book One (CHP221)
- Playing the Cello, Book One (CHP300)

Repertoire Books
- Stepping Stones for Cello (published Boosey & Hawkes)
- Waggon Wheels for Cello (published Boosey & Hawkes)
- Solo Time for Strings, Book One (published Alfred)
- String Festival Solos, Book One (published Belwin)

Sonatas/Concertinos
- Reinagle Sonatina in G Major ((published Schott)
- Breval Concertino No. 4 in C Major, arr. Feuillard (published Delrieu)
- Schaffrath Sonata in G Major (published Schott)
- Matz Sonata da Camera (published Dominis Music)
- Breval Concertino No. 5 in D Major, arr. Feuillard (published Delrieu)

Note: Books published by C. Harvey Publications are noted with an item number (CHP101) and are available at www.charveypublications.com and/or www.learnstrings.com.

©2021 C. Harvey Publications All Rights Reserved.

Step Two: Early-Intermediate Level; Starting to Shift

Methods
- Fourth Position for the Cello (CHP131) or Fourth Position Study Book for Cello (CHPD078)
- Second Position for the Cello (CHP114)
- Third Position for the Cello (CHP116)
- Suzuki Books Two and Three (if using a modified Suzuki approach) (published Summy-Birchard)

Exercises
- Finger Exercises for Cello, Book One (CHP101)
- Open-String Bow Workouts for Cello, Book One (CHP351)

Supplements and Etudes
- Squire Twelve Easy Exercises (published Stainer and Bell)
- Dotzauer 113 Studies, Book One (published International)
- Flying Fiddle Duets for Two Cellos, Book One (CHP272)
- Playing the Cello, Book Two (CHP326)
- Flying Solo Cello: Unaccompanied Folk and Fiddle Fantasias, Book One (CHP402)

Repertoire Books
- Solo Time for Strings, Book Two (published Alfred)
- String Festival Solos, Book Two (published Belwin)
- Pejtsik Violoncello Music for Beginners, Vol. 3 (published EMB)

Sonatas/Concertinos (in approximate order of study)
- **Breval Sonata in C Major (this book)**
- Marcello Sonata in E Minor (published International)

Note: Books published by C. Harvey Publications are noted with an item number (CHP101) and are available at www.charveypublications.com and/or www.learnstrings.com.

©2021 C. Harvey Publications All Rights Reserved.

Step Three: Intermediate Level; Becoming Fluent in the Lower and Neck Positions

Methods
- Fifth Position for the Cello (CHP198)
- Suzuki Books Three, Four (if using a modified Suzuki approach) (published Summy-Birchard)
- Francesconi Scuola Pratica Del Violoncello (published Suvini Zerboni)

Exercises
- Serial Shifting for the Cello (CHP106)
- Finger Exercises for Cello, Book Two (CHP130)
- Double Stop Etudes for the Cello (CHP202)

Scales
- The Two Octaves Book for Cello (CHP122)

Supplements and Etudes
- Schroeder 170 Foundation Studies, Vol. 1 (published Carl Fischer)
- Flying Fiddle Duets for Two Cellos, Book Two (CHP309)

Short Pieces
- Squire Bourree (published Carl Fischer)
- Squire Tarantella (published Carl Fischer)

Bach
- The Bach Cello Suite No. 1 Study Book (CHP332)

Sonatas/Concertos (in approximate order of study)
- Romberg Sonata in E Major Practice Edition (CHP363)
- Romberg Sonata in C Major Study Book (CHP348)
- Goltermann Concerto No. 4 Study Book for Cello (CHP364)

Note: Books published by C. Harvey Publications are noted with an item number (CHP101) and are available at www.charveypublications.com and/or www.learnstrings.com, as well as where you purchased this book.

©2021 C. Harvey Publications All Rights Reserved.

Step Four: Late-Intermediate Level; Adding Tenor Clef and the Higher Positions

Methods
- De'ak Modern Method for the Cello, Book Two (published Presser)
- Tenor Clef for the Cello (CHP109)
- Suzuki Book Five (if using a modified Suzuki approach) (published Summy-Birchard)

Exercises
- The Shifting Book for Cello, Part One (CHP171) and Part Two (CHP172)
- Shifting in Keys for Cello, Book One (CHP244)
- Double Stop Shifting for Cello (CHP219)
- Octave Shifts for the Cello, Book One (CHP104)
- Finger Exercises for Cello, Book Three (CHP142)

Scales
- Learning Three-Octave Scales on the Cello (CHP356)
- The C Major Scale Book for Cello (CHP117)
- Arpeggio Studies in Two Octaves for Cello (CHP155)

Supplements and Etudes
- Feuillard 60 Etudes for the Young Cellist (published Delrieu)
- Schroeder 170 Foundation Studies, Vol. 2 (published Carl Fischer)
- Lee 40 Melodic and Progressive Etudes, Vol. 1 (Published Schirmer)

Short Pieces
- Squire Danse Rustique (published Carl Fischer)
- Saint-Saens The Swan Study Book (CHP346)
- Saint-Saens Allegro Appassionato (published Carl Fischer)
- Faure Elegie Study Book (CHP319)

Bach
- Bach Cello Suites No. 2,3 (published Barenreiter as 6 Suites for Solo Violoncello)

Sonatas/Concertos (in approximate order of study)
- Klengel Concertino in C Major (published International)
- Romberg Sonata in G Major, Op. 43, No. 3 (published International)

Note: Books published by C. Harvey Publications are noted with an item number (CHP101) and are available at www.charveypublications.com and/or www.learnstrings.com.

©2021 C. Harvey Publications All Rights Reserved.

Also Available from C. Harvey Publications

The Romberg Sonata in E Minor Practice Edition for Cello
CHP363

- Exercises are included for difficult spots.
- Essential cello technique is distilled and presented.
- Cello part with study notes is included.
- Cello duet and piano accompaniment are both included.
- Master the Sonata that can come after the Breval C Major Sonata!

Table of Contents

Section	Page
What's In the Book	3
How to Practice Using This Edition	4
Understanding Symbols and Terms	5
Reading and Playing Half and Whole Steps	6
Preparing to Play Romberg	7
Welcome!	8
Movement One - Preparatory Exercises	9
Movement One - With Study Notes	24
Movement Two - Preparatory Exercises	28
Movement Two - Written Slower for Counting	34
Movement Two - With Study Notes	36
Movement Three - Preparatory Exercises	38
Movement Three - With Study Notes	50
Sonata in E Minor - Complete Piece	
Movement One	56
Movement Two	60
Movement Three	62
Sonata in E Minor - Cello Duet	
Movement One	66
Movement Two	72
Movement Three	74
Sonata (Cello II Part for Performance)	82
Sonata in E Minor - Piano Accompaniment	
Movement One	88
Movement Two	94
Movement Three	97
Cello Curriculum Segments - Where to Place Romberg	106

www.charveypublications.com - print books
www.learnstrings.com - downloadable books

©2021 C. Harvey Publications   All Rights Reserved.

Also Available from C. Harvey Publications

The Romberg Sonata in C Major Study Book for Cello
CHP348

- Exercises are included to teach you every measure.
- Essential cello technique is distilled and presented.
- The complete cello part to the Sonata is included.
- Master the Sonata that comes after the Romberg Sonata in E Minor!

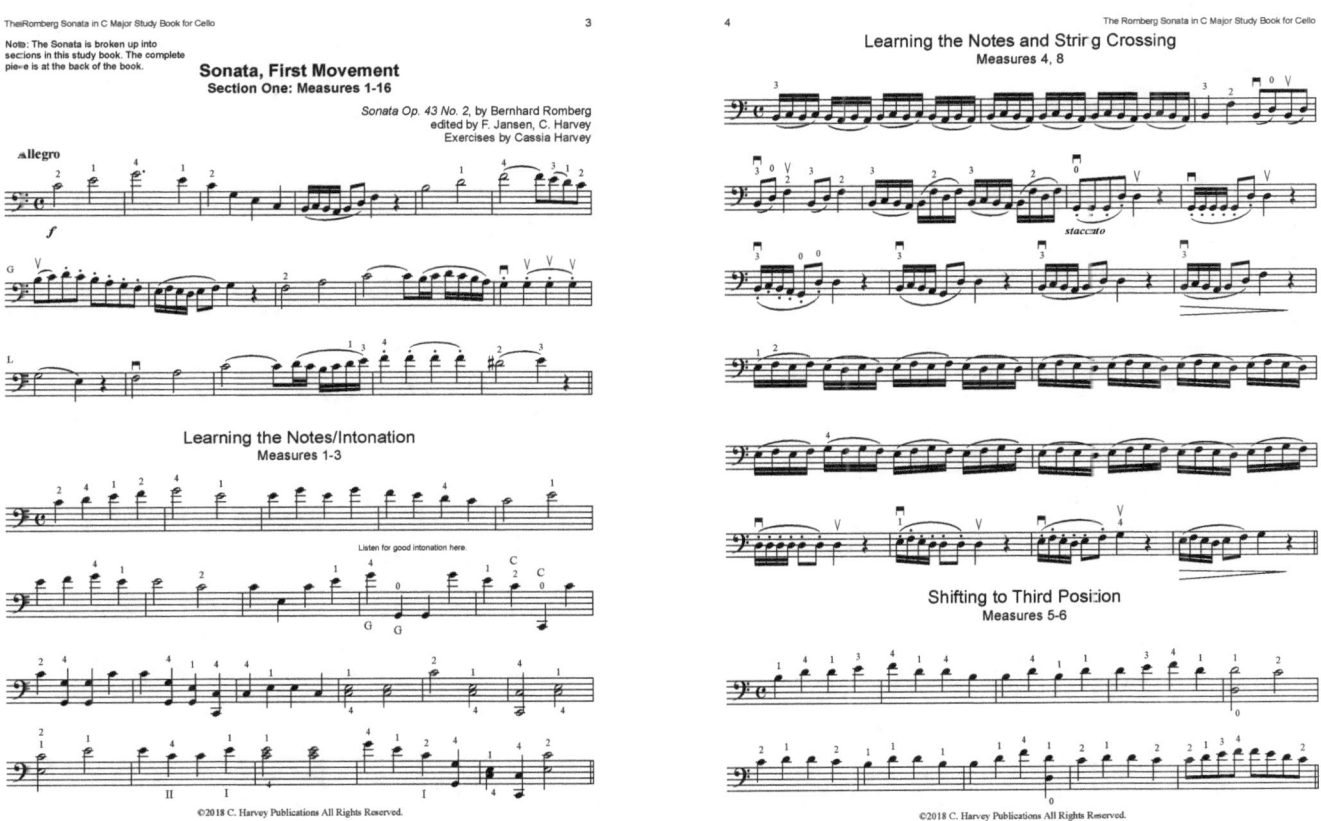

www.charveypublications.com - print books
www.learnstrings.com - downloadable books

©2021 C. Harvey Publications   All Rights Reserved.

www.ingramcontent.com/pod-product-compliance
Lightning Source LLC
Chambersburg PA
CBHW081117080526
44587CB00021B/3627